THE HOUSE OF FAITH AND FASHION

WHAT MY WARDROBE TAUGHT ME ABOUT G-D

Tobi Rubinstein

Published by Citadelle Publishing LLc
Brooklyn, New York
www.citadellebooks.com

Cover Designed by Elizabeth Sutton
Cover Photographer Rudy Arias

Copyright © 2021 Authored by Tobi Rubinstein
www.thehouseoffaithandfashion.com

All Rights Reserved.
Permission in writing must be given for all quotations or reproductions.

Printed in the United States of America
ISBN 978-0-578-87629-0
Library of Congress Control Number 2021906044
Citadelle Publishing LLc

Media Inquiries info@thehouseoffaithandfashion.com

I dedicate this book to:

My husband, Felipe Orner, for being the strength and love I have always needed.

"Te quiero con todo mi corazón."

My daughter, Lola Rubinstein, for giving me complete joy in motherhood and in life.

My cousin, Mechel Roth, for believing in me, in the special way that only a little brother could.

In loving memory of our most devoted and complete father, grandfather and great grandfather, Chaim Dov Ben Mechel Hacohen Roth (ob'm). A man full of life whose love for us was unbounded and complete in every way. A man who lived his life as his name Chaim (life).

Charitable to all who he encountered.

Heartful and dedicated in all he believed in.

Affectionate to all those he loved.

Insightful in all his feelings.

Moral in all his ways.

Our memories of you will be in our hearts always,

Sandy Roth

Mimi and Mechel Roth

Wowy and Leo Reichman and children Kiki, Pinny, Chedva, Chaim Dov and Rafoel Reichman

Toby and Yona Markowitz and children Ruvi, Tuli and Chaim Dov Markowitz

Chemy Roth

Levi Roth

The House of Faith and Fashion

The House of Faith and Fashion is a collection of essays and conversations that fuse two subjects that should be opposed to each other yet live harmoniously within these pages. The goal of this book is to reveal G-d's presence in fashion, beauty and art, viewed through the lens of Jewish teachings elevating the creative process by divine inspiration.

CONTENTS

Introduction		1
Chapter 1	Fashion	14
Chapter 2	Jewelry	74
Chapter 3	Style & Beauty	110
Chapter 4	Art	159
Chapter 5	Influencers	190
The End Is Only the Beginning		218
Acknowledgement		221

Tobi Rubinstein by Amy Martin-Friedman

"No matter how fine, noble and gifted one may be, he cannot command respect, or be appreciated by others, if he has not succeeded in realizing his talents and communicating his message to society through the medium of the creative majestic gesture."

'The Lonely Man of Faith' by Rabbi Joseph B. Soloveitchik, in Traditions Magazine 1965.

PREFACE
By: Gedale Fenster

"When grace and charm is merited then your words will penetrate into people's hearts," is an important teaching of Rabbi Nachman of Breslov. Tobi Rubinstein has achieved this goal with her book 'The House of Faith and Fashion: What my wardrobe taught me about G-d.' I have watched her path of enormous growth using her past stories as a catalyst to attain her ultimate purpose. In my years of teaching, I constantly state that one cannot reach their proper life mission without confronting the previous and/or current pain that perhaps plagues them their entire life. These are simple yet difficult steps to accomplishing the breakthrough that is needed. The first and most important one is to smash the patterns of negativity to unearth brand new patterns of rebirth and creativity. This can be accomplished by constantly fighting the tough days through firmly positioning yourself into acceptance and renewal, just as a seed in the ground that is deeply planted. These are the important tools that will help anyone pass the daily tests of life that we all receive. There is always opportunity in constriction, it is your job to find and use it. Great moments are always found in the horrible ones as G-d continues to send you the seemingly conflicted hints for you to take advantage of.

Tobi has channeled all her forces to create a book that balances the material and spiritual realms written with the charm of Chasidic teachings and her love of the Torah. With a Judaic feminine twist, she writes of Haute Couture, and the holy priestly garments, in a way that has not been approached before. We all love beautiful things, yet we need not be a slave to them, rather we should appreciate their beauty and enhancement to our lives with a G-d like presence.

Tobi has lit the way from pain to purpose in order to view both worlds with her intelligence, experience, humor and style.

INTRODUCTION

I greeted her at the door of my new house in the upper crust area known as "The Five Towns." As always, she was in her full amour of a tightly tailored, brass trimmed, Escada suit in a deep military blue. Topped off with a perfectly coiffed and lacquered shade of beauty parlor blonde, she stood with an authoritative urgency. As she perched herself on my eggplant-colored Maurice Villency leather sectional, I knew I was about to be reprimanded for wanting to divorce my husband, her only son, her prince.

"You will be nothing without my son," declared my mother-in-law in her romantic draconian accent. Although I admired her, I also noticed a slight glimmer from the small fang peeking out of her expression. I imagined a small droplet of blood there, then I quickly redirected my thoughts to the reality that I was facing a magnificent matriarch who had survived the Holocaust on her own terms.

Unbeknownst to her, the real challenge for me would have been the marching orders I expected. Did she realize that she had just given me a sort of free pass to leave and pursue a new life? Or was she just jousting for power over her son's future? I stood, facing my culinary universe of Poggenpohl cabinetry, granite landscapes and Subzero chilling stations. There appeared to be nothing lacking in my custom-built modern abode, except a true sense of self-worth. As I walked her to the teak double door entry, past the gold trimmed guest bathroom, I had the sinking but exhilarating feeling that I would never see this woman again.

My apologies, but this is not going to be my autobiography, although so many people say that I entertain them with my life story. I just wanted to get your full attention and I hopefully accomplished that by providing a tiny taste of a true story.

Let me introduce myself. I am Tobi Rubinstein, the most authentic version of myself to date.

I will start from the beginning and hopefully you can understand, sympathize, empathize, celebrate, and relate to my journey to elevate fashion, art, and culture to a spiritual level.

In my senior high school yearbook from Bais Yaakov of Queens, I was voted "most likely to shop." That will give you the foundation of my priorities then. Somewhere around 9th grade, I found my inner fashion frequency, which probably coincided with the discovery of boys. Since I attended an all-girls religious school, boys and careers were not the emphasis of my education. Their educational goal was to groom girls to become wives and mothers. In contrast, my parents were entangled in a vicious divorce, which set an entirely different example for me than my yeshiva (Hebrew school). Twisted up in the humiliating scandal of my parents, while trying to uphold Judaic values for young women, proved to be more than challenging for me. I discovered the key to my survival would always be looking the part, as if my outfit were my suit of armor against the public. Saving all my babysitting money to buy "the" green bamboo print wrap dress from Diane Von Furstenberg (the late 70's) proved to me that I could feel sane if I were cloaked in the latest fashion. Little did I know how prophetic that would be for my career and personal life.

I could just print my resume here, but that would be boring because the best stories are always between the lines. Since I had already established my love for clothes, I entered the Fashion Institute of Technology, majoring in Fashion Buying and Merchandising. It was thrilling to be in a school that lived, breathed, and slept in bolts of luscious fabric and rainbows of threads and trim. But my family situation would not allow my dream education to continue, so dropped out and got married instead.

Moving to the Midwest with my new husband, I got my first real job in a luxury boutique which seemed to specialize in Big Ten Football games and country club lunches. I am laughing as I remember wearing my Betsey

Introduction

Johnson animal skin jumpsuit on my first day of work where I received very puzzled looks. Three years later, I had learned to dress window mannequins, sell Spartan green wool suits, accessorize Izod's and worship Ralph Lauren.

Returning to New York, I quickly adapted back to Maud Frizon shoes and Giorgio Sant Angelo silk dresses. My homecoming job was with a maternity company. Going from retail into wholesale was a transition that landed me straight in the heart of the garment district. Starting as a receptionist, I quickly climbed the ladder to Vice President of Sales traveled to all the fashion markets and industry shows. My first marriage ended just as I turned 30 and hit what seemed to be the height of my career. Did one have anything to do with the other? Yes, no, and maybe.

The company went bankrupt after it was sold to an aviation conglomerate for its real estate value, and I was left unemployed. Next stop was a private label manufacturer with offices in the infamous 1407 Broadway building and I entered marriage number 2. At Third Generation my fashion education was stretched beyond my dreams. Since they were one of the main suppliers for Victoria's Secret and JC Penney, I learned all about private label, creating catalogs, line sheets, fabric purchases and sales projections. But the most important lessons were in relationships and appearances. Traveling to Dallas to visit corporate headquarters required an assortment of Christian Lacroix, Gemma Kahng and Donna Karan power suits along with my oversized black Chanel tote loaded with files (pre internet). Paris and Milan were my favorite stops as I shopped the stores for trends and FedExed samples back to NYC in time to copy and present them at my next corporate merchandising meeting.

I accepted a partnership with another private label manufacturer that wanted to start licensing popular brands. Crunch Gyms was just emerging as a fitness contender and I jumped at the chance to license their in-house activewear. I knew my plate might be full, yet I overloaded myself with another brand extension at Nicole Miller for Kids. While I was pricing their exclusive collection for Bloomingdales one day, I realized how overwhelmed I felt with a new baby, uncooperative partners, and a sinking feeling of failure. I will never forget my conversation with Nicole Miller as I was about to resign. She could not understand why I wanted to give up. Was it the hormones or the misunderstood males that surrounded me? When I think back to my discussion with her, I realize that she had more faith in my ability than I had in myself.

I gave up and did the Mommy thing which happily became the greatest success of my life. But my creative spirit never stopped calling. Since licensing seemed like an easy way back into the fashion market, I reentered it with The Rubinstein Group. I took on projects for BUM Equipment, Ocean Pacific, Disney, and Universal Studios. I almost fainted at the chance to develop a fragrance for Jenifer Lopez called, "Emperitise." At that time, I met a pair of amazingly talented women who thoroughly understood my drive. We bonded over an attempted acquisition of Gottex Swimwear to be resurrected using Christy Brinkley as the new spokesperson.

As I continued to work with these women, we discovered a void in the market. Hip Hop culture was rising faster than any trend with Phat Farm, Fubu and Southpole rocketing, and we wanted in on the action. To set us apart we created our own brand called, "Ched-da," (slang for money) and marketed it exclusively to Kmart. You could say that I got my MBA from that experience. Three little girls going up against the male-dominated mass market industry was a daunting task and I did it while also dealing with an unsupportive husband. The effort was well received at Kmart.

The Detroit Free Press business section broke the story in the summer of 2002,

"Move over Sean Jean and Phat Farm. There is a new urban clothing line, and it is only available at

*Kmart Corp. stores.

On Sept. 1, 50 stores in New York, New Jersey, Ohio, Pennsylvania and Washington, D.C., will test a new men's clothing line called Ched-da. Slang

for money, Ched-da is described as a young man's urban, hip-hop line a New York company created for the mass market.

Make no mistake, this is not a tricked-out version of Kmart's Route 66 clothing line. Think FUBU and Mecca, but at a discount.

"You can be cool, and you don't have to spend a lot of money," said Tobi Rubinstein, president of Ched-da. "I'm no different than Sean John. I'm just $9.99."

That story was picked up all over the US.

We had a party, while it lasted, with marketing campaigns in **XXL Magazine**, a Ched-da branded Brink's truck throwing out cash to crowds in Las Vegas, HBO's "The Wire" cast members and the official sponsor of the TV series "Hip Hop Nation." Ched-da was soon voted one of the top 50 brands of the decade in **Vibe Magazine**, which gave it the street credibility we coveted.

Then, the ever-revolving CEOs at Kmart crashed our party, and we could not find a new home for the brand in that tumultuous retail world. We reluctantly shut our doors. I felt the failure in both the business and the ending of marriage number 2.

Marriage number 3 came with a husband and a job, a duality that I hoped would be a combination I could handle. Little did I know what awaited me and the high price I would pay.

I became a very public Rebbetzin (Rabbi's wife) to a "celebrated" congregation in a wealthy summer community on Long Island.

I quickly learned that my outfit and shoes were more important than whether I knew how to pray properly. My Carolina Herrera suits, and Manolo Blahnik shoes were studied intensely as I walked to the front row every Shabbos morning. I unexpectedly created a fashion monster, setting the standard for the congregation to strive for at this celebrity institution. To further define myself, I started a ministry of my own, "The House of Faith and Fashion," where faith and fashion could coexist harmoniously. Since this "House" was always my address, I decided to invite the congregation over for a visit.

In the press release, The House of Faith and Fashion Party was slated as "the most exclusive Hamptons event of the season of summer 2009," complete with celebrity hosts and guests. After 20 models walked the runway in my spacious backyard, I announced my intention and mission to have inspiring conversations about the balance between the spiritual and material world with leaders in both the faith and fashion communities. They would be targeted to explore style, substance, and faith. I would intertwine faith and fashion, two topics usually considered incompatible. They would be entertaining and thought-provoking conversations. I started with my most popular question for any fashion icon, "Do you believe that your talent is G-d given?"

The second event proved newsworthy when found in **The NY Post's** Page Six column because I asked Douglas Hannant a tricky question by inquiring into the style choices of our nation's First Ladies. Well, I think I angered the White House because the poor designer had to issue a formal apology!

I interviewed Mark Badgley and James Mischka in their beautiful new store on Worth Ave. in Palm Beach, FL. As my interviews increased, I was fascinated by the depth of faith I found in many important fashion leaders.

Well, the story could have ended right there when I became "just another ex-wife" again. But this time, my new name on the street and in the press was "Wife #4." It was personally devastating and very public.

I felt like Alice in Wonderland as she fell down the rabbit hole. The rooms in my life were grossly out of proportion. There were Mad Hatters disguised as public relations firms and crazy Queens dressed up as therapists. There were sly cats camouflaged as friends and tea parties known as media outlets. It was a long and scary journey back to the right side of the mirror with the help of many G-d appointed angels that saved my life and my mind.

At my lowest point, Rebbetzin Esther Jungreis placed me in a private grief management group where I met a woman who was a Rabbi in the same Long Island enclave of the rich and famous. She made a huge impression on me. It changed the direction of my life.

I remember clearly the first night of Chanukah 2011, when I went to visit my "modern Bobov Chassidish" family in Boro Park (Brooklyn) for our usual holiday party. I announced my desire to go to seminary to become a Rabbi. My uncle Chaim Roth jumped up from his seat and proclaimed "Toba Leah, if you want to study Torah after what you just went through, I'm 100% for it." Clearly this was not an acceptable professional choice for women in orthodox Jewish circles, but I felt an urgency to have the Rabbi title to redefine myself. I admit that it came with a lot of misinterpretations and confusion, only being understood outside of my circle. My uncle slammed his fists on the table as a judge with a gavel and handed me my permission with love. In his infinite wisdom, he knew I would learn and grow to love my religion more than ever. Mitzvah gorreret Mitzvah? (One good deed leads to another.) Even my father, Abe Roth, approved of my ambition and wanted to practice my weekly sermons with me. In the last months of his life, he told everyone that no other Rabbi had taught him more Torah than his own daughter. It was an important time in my relationship with my father that I will never forget.

I laugh at it now, but revenge was my initial driving force for graduating JSLI (Jewish Spiritual Leadership Seminary- online Rabbinical and Cantorial school), which trains clergy for the modern world. I was not interested in doing everything a male Rabbi did, I only wanted the title and what I believed would be a new direction. After graduation, as Rabbi Tobi Rubinstein, I moved forward with my dream of the "House of Faith and Fashion."

With a hugely talented crew, headed by Derrick Hammond (now a renowned movie director, CEO/Founder of 20/20 Vizion Entertainment), we produced 10 episodes of "The House of Faith and Fashion TV Show" for NBC Nonstop Media that never actually aired. But filming the show gave me access to fashion royalty such as Patricia Field, famed stylist for "Sex in The City," who taught me the true meaning of humility. The series failure was huge for me. Faith combined with fashion was a concept ahead of its time. At times I have believed my entire existence has been out of sync with the times.

Next, I moved into radio, with the team behind Geraldo Rivera producing my weekly "The House of Faith and Fashion Radio Show," on Blog Talk Radio. I interviewed guests from various industries like real estate, sports, fashion, stockbrokers, even shampoo makers, always bringing in an element of faith to our discussion.

This led me to guest spots as a Fashion and Faith Commentator on major news outlets like ABC, Huffington Post, The New York Post, I24, Lifetime, and Arise.

Eventually, the unpleasant taste of a cocktail of bills and reality hit me, and I shelved "The House of Faith and Fashion." Surprisingly, in my personal life, the Rabbi role began to gain substance. Suddenly I was getting calls from women who desperately wanted to talk to a female Rabbi about their issues in marriage, betrayal, abuse, and abandonment. Each of them hoped that because I had survived my own marital traumas and revitalized my faith, that I could genuinely relate to their needs. My friends started to call me, "The Faith Fixer." I knew the exact pain a woman was feeling by looking at her face because I recognized the same emptiness and struggle in myself.

As I comforted more and more women of diverse faith backgrounds, I began to realize how important my ministry would be and the reason it was so relevant. I felt the urgency to study Torah again, only this time I wanted to learn what, why, when, where and how, which I never quite learned at

Introduction

Yeshivah Bais Yackov of Queens or in seminary. I wanted to truly know my faith and what it meant at a much deeper level. I wholeheartedly began to study again.

In the summer of 2014, a close friend approached me about the controversial New York Horse and Carriages political issue. After visiting the stables and meeting the union heads, I had a crazy dream about producing the wildest New York Fashion Week show. A friend and I formed "The Tahor Group" as a boutique marketing firm. We kicked off an "Opening Ceremony," for New York Fashion Week the likes of which New York has never seen before. With the help of the NYPD, the Teamsters Union officials, and top real estate moguls, we shut down Central Park South to hold a moving fashion show with models in horse drawn carriages dressed in the debut 2015 Collections. We had no idea it would get the crazy amount of press coverage it received globally. We had over 90 million media impressions.

'Fashion Week is getting off to a galloping start.' - **New York Daily News**

'...was described as a moveable fashion show through the Park.' - **Daily Mail UK**

'New York Fashion Week Spring 2015 launched...with models in Central Park Horse and Carriages.' - **Associated Press**

'...staged a different kind of runway celebrating everything New York as he kicked off Fashion Week a day early giving people plenty to talk about.' - **CNN**

'Models wearing a new collection travel in a parade of horse-drawn carriages along 59th street in Manhattan on Wednesday.' - **The Wall Street Journal**

'seven models in horse-drawn carriages Wednesday night for a moveable fashion show through Central Park.' - **New York Times**

From there, The Tahor Group went on to produce numerous fashion marketing extravaganzas with top New York and Israeli designers. We showed the excitement of the "back and front of the house" with models, makeup and hair teams, agents, press and dressers, photographers and handlers and it was worth all the hard work. The last fashion show we produced was in 2017 showcasing the Negev desert as a loving and magnificent tribute to Israel's creativity.

As time went on, I got older, and the dating scene got younger. After an assortment of relationship fiascos that resulted in renewed issues of low self-worth, my dearest friend, Chanie Einhorn introduced me to Gedale Fenster. I certainly credit him and his daily lectures for putting me on the right track and teaching me to "stay in my lane," which is his tag line. He taught me to relook at my past trauma and become my new improved self. He counseled me to divorce my past and marry my future. Sure enough, that is exactly what I did!

You should have seen my fourth husband, the handsome and wonderful, Felipe Orner, and his family's reaction, when I delivered a dvar Torah (a talk based on Torah) at our wedding about the importance of the number "4" in Judaism. It was not what they expected from a woman in a Carolina Herrera gown!

Moving back to Queens after leaving at 19 years old, was like being unearthed from a time capsule. I found myself living a few blocks from where I was raised. I started writing a column for the local newspaper and I reintroduced myself to my old neighborhood. Each week I would introduce a point of art, culture or fashion and fuse it with Torah (bible) for my articles.

This book is my personal Megillah (story) and a whole lot more.

I wish I could stop right the story right here but there is more.

Introduction

G-d had another plan for me that disrupted 2020. During the High Holidays, after recuperating from a hip replacement in early August, I was not feeling right. After sitting at Synagogue services, masked up and unable to find a comfortable position for myself, I saw a series of doctors to discover the source of my pain. Continuing extensive and invasive medical tests showed conflicting results for the fluid that had found a home in my chest cavity. Finally, a biopsy and PET scan gave me the dreadful answer. Hearing the news that I have Stage IV Mullerian cancer of the uterus and ovaries was NOT a chapter I was in any way, shape or form prepared for.

I was filled with questions. Haven't I been through enough already? I just got married in 2018 to the man who should have always been my husband, erasing the all the difficult years spent before him. Didn't I deserve the happy home that I was finally in? What did I do wrong that I have not already paid for in family fiascos, failed marriages, disastrous divorces, and busted businesses?

I consulted with Breslov's Rabbi Shalom Arush and begged for a plan to help me understand and question G-d about his love for me while retaining my gratitude. I engaged all my religious and holistic contacts desperate to find an answer. There is a gospel song from the movie, "The Color Purple" called "G-d is tryin' to tell u something" that went on a loop in my head as I tried to make any of sense out of this diagnosis.

G-d gives you a purpose in life and He keeps reminding you of His will, no matter who or where you are. He sends almost constant messages. If you do not listen, He will continue until you do!

I finally listened this time as His signal was directed straight to my soul through a potentially deadly disease, cancer.

Now I am unpacking and repacking my new life journey along with this book as my written guide. With G-d's mercy, my hopes are to convey messages of strength, faith, and love, while building a great new chapter for the rest of my life.

Welcome to my home, "The House of Faith and Fashion."

CHAPTER 1
FASHION

"In embroidered apparel she will be brought to the king"
Psalms 45: 15

The House of Faith and Fashion

Model: Armani Jones
Photo courtesy of Fashion Week Studio

Haute and Holy

The first Monday in May is always fashion's biggest night out. The Met Ball, in honor of the Metropolitan Museum of Art Costume Institute exhibit's opening season is the Oscars ceremony of fashion. The red carpet is a brand placement machine, parading A-List entertainment personalities, playing high end brand ambassadors. At a very steep ticket prices, fashion finds fortune and fame. Over the years, I have watched and commented on TV about this grand speculator with awe, respect, and admiration. There were times that the exhibits were so stunning that they brought me to tears, leaving me unable to fully comprehend their beauty. I needed to view them at least three times to see all their intricate details, certainly the case with "Alexander McQueen and China: Through the Looking Glass."

Several years ago, the Met presented the "Heavenly Bodies" exhibit. It was so grand it occupied both the Met on 5th Avenue and its uptown location at the Cloisters. According to "The Art Newspaper" article, "New York has clinched the top two spots in our list of the world's most popular exhibitions in 2018 with the double blockbusters: "Heavenly Bodies: Fashion and the Catholic Imagination," which received around 10,900 visitors a day across two venues." As with every exhibit, it was meticulously curated by Andrew Bolton and knighted by Anna Wintour, Editor in Chief of "Vogue." The Catholic-centric fashion collection ran from its designated hall downstairs and flowed through the Lehman wing. Then effortlessly continued at the Cloisters, the museum's peaceful home for religious art in Manhattan. The exhibit included historical fashion figures like Elsa Schiaparelli, Balenciaga, Christian Lacroix and Yves Saint Laurent, and active designers like Jean Paul Gaultier, John Galliano, and Raf Simons. After spending hours mesmerizingly viewing each section of true fashion genius, it reminded me of a conference I attended in Madrid (2008) that was hosted by King Juan Carlos of Spain and late King Abdullah of Saudi Arabia.

They jointly invited all heads of religions, Catholic to Coptic, from around the world to partake in a global spiritual initiative. My mind nearly exploded with the assortment of supremely luxurious ceremonial religious attire accessorized with incomparable ornate jewelry. Golden lace with crowns of rubies and sapphires were strewn across the room. It is funny because I noticed that the Rabbis in attendance were the worst dressed in mere suits and ties.

Long before Catholicism or The Met ever existed, the concept of divinity in costume was conceived by G-d. Do they know the very first master couturier was G-d himself? The Kohen Gadol's (High Jewish Priest) majestic attire rivals and far surpasses any mortal design by the most highly acclaimed fashion houses of Paris and Milan. The intricate detaila of lace, color, embroidery, and jewels had mastery far above any museum exhibit. Do we ever stop to think of Torah (Bible) and how it relates to fashion? Two subjects void of each other, or so it might seem. "Some might consider fashion to be an unfitting or unseemly medium by which to engage with ideas about the sacred or the divine," claims Andrew Bolton. A statement that I strongly disagree with.

I always found it puzzling that of all industries to be schooled by G-d himself after the Egyptian exile, it would be garment manufacturing. Living in the dessert, the Jewish people were provided with food or manna from the heavens, water from Miriam's well, along with a special cloud of protection. Why did He choose the fashioning of His priests as one of the first hands on learning experiences?

The subject along with detailed instructions are introduced in the Torah (Bible) portion Tetzaveh, filling the entirety of Exodus 28. They are described again in detail in Pekudei (Exodus 39:1–31) as well.

The divinely designed costume of the High Priest consisted of many intricate parts. The Me'il or robe was worn on top of the linen tunic ensemble (worn by all Kohanim) and was woven entirely out of precious sky-blue wool. Trimmed with chiming "pomegranates" of sky blue, purple, and crimson red wool. The ephod was a vest or cape-like garment that had a richly embroidered patterns made from threads spun of gold, sky-blue, purple, crimson red wool, and twined linen. Worn on top of the robe, it had two shoulder straps upon each of which was placed a precious onyx stone set in gold. Upon these two stones were engraved the names of the twelve tribes of Israel.

Extending from the shoulder straps of the ephod were two cables of solid gold from which was suspended the breastplate, or "'Choshen." This ornament was fashioned out of a piece of material woven after the manner of the ephod. It was doubled over, and on its surface twelve gold settings were placed. In each of the settings was a precious stone associated with one of the tribes. The three rows were adorned with sapphires, emeralds, amethyst, turquoise and topaz, which outshines master jewelers such as Bulgari, Tiffany and Van Cleef & Arpels. Within the doubled fold of the breastplate was placed the mysterious "Urim veTumim," a hidden "designer label.

Finally, we have the "Tzitz" or headband that the Ramban understands as a type of crown. Made from pure gold, it was inscribed with two words "Kodesh LaHashem" or "Holy to G-d." The ordinary priests had four garments, a tunic, breeches, a turban, and a sash.

Four of these garments are worn exclusively by the High Priest. They alone are called bigdai kodesh (the holy garments). Moses first places them upon Aaron at the consecration of the priests (Leviticus 8:7–9). Aaron wears them until his death, transferring them to his son and successor Eleazar immediately before he dies (Numbers 20:25–28). All successive High Priests are commanded to wear them as well (Exodus 29:30; see Leviticus 21:10).

The world of art, culture and design should pay homage to the world's first and foremost couturier, G-d.

Masking Fashion

This is a time to examine the content of what we are reading, writing, seeing, and doing. It causes me to question my own mission of The House of Faith and Fashion,, where I combine art, culture and fashion with Torah (Bible) based teachings. Currently, the arena of creativity in humankind has given way to a crisis of human nature. My hopes are still to find meaning in my fusion and to educate and entertain.

Let us consider the required medical turned fashion accessory of our current time, the mask. It has unleashed a new world of "must haves" with creativity, wit, and social consciousness. High end designers like Gucci, Ralph Lauren, Marni, and Louis Vuitton offer them as well as crafty home sewn versions that are blowing up Etsy shops. The common theme is the global pandemic requires them so why not make them pretty since they occupy a good portion of everyone's face. It is also a means for fashion business not to be left on the shelf.

At the start of this trend, my dear friend, Eyal Assulin, famed Israeli artist and sculptor, designed a group of face masks. Since I know that he does not create out of boredom, I contacted him to see what his message was. With Eyal there is always a deep message.

Tobi, "Why do you think that masks are so fashionable?"

Eyal, "I think masks became so fashionable thanks to the mystery it creates our ability to visually and physically cover half of our face and stay attractive and intriguing and actually more intriguing than we are fully exposed. There is something about the act of concealment that generates greater curiosity about the person who wears it. Artistically, the mask functions as another layer of that person, that is, the type of facial extension and extension of the persona he represents."

Tobi, "Where does G-d fit in with a mask?"

Eyal, "To me, the mask's connection to G-d is our ability to cover the organ of speech, our mouth, and to create an inner silence that allows us to listen. Have you ever heard your breathing out of the mask like an echo coming back from you? The resulting acoustics allow us to listen to the speech and breath more than usual."

Tobi, "Is there a meaning to your collection as opposed to the "designer label" masks that high society is wearing?"

Eyal, "The mask is an accessory and yet very individual, each person will buy a mask according to the person he represents. The masks I make WFH (COVID-19 quarantine) are different, and each is one of a kind. Visually, it functions as a mirror to the contemporary era in which people trade masks like stolen diamonds, a contemporary post-capitalism crisis. Since fashion often reflects the sign of the times, is there a much deeper message here as well."

Without going into the political or capitalistic approach, Eyal touched a big Torah (Bible) topic in the covering, concealing, and limiting the mouth to an internal silence. Which has played itself out dangerously over the course of elections, racial causes, conspiracy theories, faux news outlets, and dark internet sites.

"Death and Life lay in the hand of the tongue," (Proverbs 18:21), warned King Solomon. Hebrew has two words for language, lashon and safah. These two words, Rabbi Avraham Yitzchak Kook explained, correspond to two aspects of speech, the inner meaning of our words (inside of the mouth) or the message we intend to communicate and our external "attire" (the lips). Then, how our words are interpreted by others, which include posts, comments, and tweets. "If we do not express ourselves clearly, our words will fail to convey our true intent," says Rav Kook.

There are two major pitfalls in speech, and we pray to Hashem (G-d) for guidance and clarity of what is correct and what is truly harmful. The first concerns the inner content of our words. The other is the huge terrain of proper and harmless communication to others which is a slippery slope to grave harm to others. What comes out of your mouth can destroy worlds.

You can explore this further with Rabbi Akiva Tatz's book, **Worldmask**, which contains the keys to unlock the spiritual world that exists behind the mask of the physical. The relationship of the inner to the outer soul, and human to G-d.

We wear masks during Purim time. I often say that when I put on makeup, I feel like I am putting on a Kabuki mask. Kabuki is a form of Japanese classical theater known for its elaborate costumes and dynamic acting. We all put on masks in some form or another. Admitting that, the mask we wear now is a gravely important one. It is a form of protection against the virus outside, and a form of protection against what is inside. Or is it the great balancing tool to get the outside and inside to work together as one? We must be cautious to stop spreading the virus and be as cautious with what we say to each other, on the internet, social media and even to ourselves, because G-d is listening.

The White Party

GQ magazine has hailed Mr. Sean Combs AKA Diddy's annual summer White Party as a Hampton's social season knockout. "Since its inception in the '90s, the event has always been a showstopper." From Mary J. Blige to Maria Carey, all the star-studded guests wear white at his annual event. According to fashion experts throughout the ages, your white wardrobe has been given permission to be worn starting Memorial Day till Labor Day.

I lovingly remember the days of Shavuot at The Concord Hotel in the Catskills in my youth. There were a parade of white outfits going down the makeshift runway that approached the main dining hall entry. While visiting Rio De Janeiro, Brazil on a holiday in 1991, I witnessed an entirely white New Year's Eve celebration. The Macumba ceremony is a form of white magic voodoo religious practice where thousands of people swarm the beaches, wearing only white, with white flowers and candles. Although

I do not understand any of this, except it is absolutely forbidden in the Torah (Bible), the vast sea of white left a big impression on me.

Back in Emily Post's era, when dress code rules where the only proper way to live, the "summer season" was bracketed by Memorial Day and Labor Day. High Society ladies flocked from town houses to their seaside "cottages" or mountain "cabins" to escape the heat. City clothes were left exchanged for lighter, whiter, summer outfits. This fashion code of law christened wearing white as the official start of warm weather fun in the sun. A carefree canvas that had yet to be painted with a summer full of life.

Coincidently, Shavuot falls close to Memorial Day weekend, sometimes at the same time. The parading of crisp white attire is not only found in this secular start of the season, but white clothes also have a celebratory role in the special holiday of Matan Torah, Shavuot.

In Israel, the pioneers of the early 20th century who reclaimed the land refocused the meaning of Shavuot with the agricultural aspects of the holiday. In modern Bikkurim festivals children dressed in white, carried baskets filled with produce from their local villages and kibbutzim (communal farms) in their grand parade. They were reading poems, singing, dancing, and displaying artwork, which were sold to benefit the early days of The Jewish National Fund. This organization is known in Hebrew as Keren Kayemet le-Yisrael, a fund created to purchase land from Arab landowners with the ultimate plan of settling Jewish pioneers on it. Its main goal was successfully establishing the State of Israel. Until today, there are similar festivals taking place around the country.

In many Sephardic congregations, prior to the Torah (Bible) reading on the first day of Shavuot, a ketubah le-Shavuot (marriage certificate for Shavuot) is read as a symbolic betrothal of G-d and His people. The premarital document specifying the conditions agreed upon between the two parties, or the ketubah which is a certificate the bridegroom presents to the bride at the wedding ceremony. Wearing white is a symbol of the bride and groom's symbolic marriage that G-d makes with the children of

Israel during this holiday. My dear friend Rabbanit Dr Adena Berkowitz explains the white attire for Shavuot as, "Like the bridal dress at a wedding the spiritual marriage of the Jewish people with Hashem (G-d). The Torah (Bible) is the ketibah."

According to Aish TLV Rabbi Shlomo Chen for YNET news, "Wearing white is basically like being an angel. Basically, we are dressing like angels. We are returning to Eden, where the same concept of only eating milk products or vegetables and fruits is that we're all pure."

Hashem (G-d) gifted us the wisdom of the world through the Torah (Bible) allowing us to reach spiritual levels of the highest order, where, we are in no need of any particular color. We have a clean canvas on which a story is yet to be painted. The acceptance of the Torah (Bible) has given us a fresh start without any prejudice of past color palettes.

Wearing white could have started in the beginning of Eretz Yisrael (state of Israel) pioneering days or in the interpretation of wedding outfits as bride and groom receiving the Torah (Bible). Wearing white could be a symbol of a clean slate of consciousness, after 49 days of personal growth, from the depths of impurity to the pinnacle of divine purity. White is the height of perfection, which is the meaning of Shavuot. To be able to embrace the Torah (Bible) at the height of perfection equals perfection in Hashem's (G-d's) timing to give us the Torah (Bible) as his perfectly chosen people, perhaps dressed in white at G-d's white party.

I Have Nothing to Wear

I am not sure if I should say the blessing of "Shehechiyanu," on my first day of chemotherapy. It is the mini prayer, "Who has given us life?" It is a common Jewish prayer to celebrate first time special occasions designed to express gratitude to G-d for new and unusual experiences.

It is a sad but good question to ask a rabbi. There is no coincidence either that today is Rosh Chodesh (new month), Tevet, day 6 of Chanukah and the beginning of my journey down the rabbit hole of stage IV Mullerian cancer.

As I lay here, tucked into a hospital bed, sporting the functional jewelry of an IV hookup, I feel the weight of the path that led me here. After three months of a labyrinth of medical tests and a buffet of doctors, I was diagnosed with this illness. Riding a Ferris wheel of emotions, I finally got the correct answer, and the game plan to get on the next ride, which seems more like a monster rollercoaster.

I have NOTHING to wear for this. There is no invitation that states the dress code. No seasonal rules, no modesty requirements, no proper protocol instructions. There is absolutely nothing to prepare yourself.

I am reminded of a deep teaching in the Tanya (chapter 4, section 2) about garments of a different sort. The soul possesses three auxiliary powers, (thought, speech, and action) which are instruments of expression. Like garments, they can be worn or discarded. When the soul embraces any of these three powers, it is "clothed" or draped in these attributes. When it chooses not to utilize them, it is "undressed. As garments give definition to the wearer's beauty and importance so too the soul is glamourized (beautified) by the attire of these powers.

My uniform for this war is made of thought, speech and action, a trio of enlightened design directors for The TSA Collection worn by the best of souls at the worst of times. Maybe I can launch a marketing campaign. My mind is visualizing all kinds of creative outlets now because I unknowingly already started last night.

Putting together another WhatsApp group of friends could crash my phone but I had the idea to assemble my front-line friends to arrange a Torah (Bible) lecture the night before each of my chemotherapy sessions. My intention is to fuse, fortify, and fashion my army to be ready for the fight along with me.

On the softer side, I also feel like I am being enveloped by a magical, meaningful, and spiritual quilt. Each person adding a special piece to the beautiful blanket stitched together with a common unbreakable faith in G-d. Comfortably cradled in my hospital bed at Mount Sinai in Manhattan NY, I closed my eyes and had a vision concerning the fluid bag that is in military maneuvers. My special quilt is made up of a lifetime of cherished relationships being sewn together with the experience of a master tailor on Saville Row. Two bags of the medicinal cocktail are the liquid glue keeping it all together.

I am reminded of Joseph's jealousy inducing colorful coat when visualizing my quilt. If I blink three times like Samantha on "Bewitched" maybe I can wear it as I sashay down the runway to the door out of this hospital.

"The Long Haul to Health" is embroidered into the right edge of the fabric to remind me how durable my friends made it.

Could it be that this cancer is just here to make sure I complete this book? You know what they say about G-d's signs. He keeps sending them until you get the message. There is nothing like being told you have cancer to kick yourself into gear.

My thoughts drift to many "back of the house" New York Fashion Weeks, a term meaning the preparations for a runway show. There is so much to do to send your collection out to the world. Models, and dressers, assistants and agents, makeup and beauty directors, lighting and loading music, madness, press, and tons of people are up front in the back.

Could this be a metaphor for my comfy blanket and colorful coat that G-d has arranged my friends and family to sew? They warn you that you get "Chemo Brain", and your memory can feel depleted. I am forgetting my train of thought more times than I want to admit.

My quilt is made up of cute emojis, thoughtful texts, words of faith and healing, zoom rooms, and FaceTime, gifts of caftans, and lipstick, and hearts filled with love towards me and G-d. Could you picture any cloth more magnificent than that?

When I close my eyes, I can see the frenzy and flurries of a New York Fashion Week show. However, this time the focus is on the perfectly styled selections for my soul to wear, the Ready to Wear (RTW) collection for The TSA (Thought, Speech, Action) label.

The venue is packed, the front row is loaded, the lineup is formed, the music is ready, the director whispers, "3,2,1, walk Tobi, walk."

Sustainability Is a Recycled Idea

When I looked at the label of my new blue camouflage puffer coat from Zara, I was a bit startled. Usually, a coat like this is made of goose down feathers and nylon, this one was composed of recycled water bottles. As explained by Zara, "This plastic is collected within 50 km of waterways and coastal areas without a formal collection infrastructure at the Rivera Maya coast. Zara continues its mission of repurposed fashion in a partnership with the Council of Fashion Designers in America (CFDA) and challenged four designers to create an outfit that is half vintage upcycled fashion and part new fabric. Nine pieces were created, including a tie-dye slip dress by Alejandra Alonso Rojas, a layered pink three-piece linen suit by Private Policy and a patchwork linen trench coat by Barragán. There are several more companies that have jumped on board the trend. Levi's launched

SecondHand, its first resale offering, and H&M opened Looop, which it described as the world's first in-store garment-to-garment recycling system.

The terminology of "repurpose" and "sustainability" is the latest fixation of the industry. It utilizes all kinds of used, tossed, thrown out, overage, garbage and trash to be reborn into a brand-new clothing item. According to "Vogue" there are an estimated 50 million tons of clothing discarded every year, and most of it will not biodegrade in a landfill.

The amount of time, energy, and resources that go into those trashed items is usually disproportionate to their lighting speed turnaround. A single cotton T-shirt has a noticeably short closet life cycle. One person's trash is now becoming another's treasure.

I could refer to her as the Mary Poppins of revamped vintage, but Kate Mcguire's Converted Closet is a pandora's box of fashion goodies with a deep spiritual soul and a great British accent. Her Instagram is filled with fun transformations of finds that magically turn into couture pieces designed or reconstructed by Kate and her crew of merry dressmakers. After submitting my two worn out Burberry coats to be whipped into a new rendition, I got into a conversation with her about my book.

Kate's profound take on fashion was deeply rooted in faith. She was speaking my language.

Tobi, "Do you believe that your talents are G-d given?"

Kate McGuire, "Absolutely and what a relief! My belief is that there is a constant flow of inspiration and know-how available at all times, if one stays connected; it is my biggest thrill, knowing that the loving source is bigger than me and can never be switched off. It is deeply empowering and energizing."

Tobi, "Does each conversion speak to you spiritually? Is there Genesis moment of creation that happens with each piece?"

Kate McGuire, "To me, all things on earth are comprised of energy and clothes are so precious as they sit directly on our skin. They are the closest thing physically to us during our waking hours. The clothes I convert talk to me. My dressmaker in London will confirm this because she started to witness it over time, tuned in herself. I begin the conversion process by putting the garment on in front of a mirror and asking myself what clothes I see hidden inside. As the ideas start to flow, I move the garment around to see what it would potentially look like in the various forms it could take to see if one lights me up. And yes, there is always a Genesis moment of creation, a sartorial epiphany. My dressmakers and I chat about the incredible thrill of conversion. It is a spiritual experience because it's pure creativity in action."

Tobi, "How do you think sustainability, recycling and upcycling have their roots in faith?"

Kate McGuire, "I believe the issue of climate change is one we will eventually solve. This is what human beings have done throughout the course of history, work together to find solutions to seemingly insurmountable, dire situations. In the drive to find necessary solutions, new heights of creativity are reached. In our drive to create a sustainable fashion industry, we must completely rethink every moment of a garment's existence, from supply chain to end-of-life. In my view, the fashion landscape will look radically different in 10 years. It will be fueled with much more unique, original fashion, created by many more home-designers and makers, using the billions of clothes already in existence. Consumers will automatically consider conversion as an alternative to buying new when seeking fabulous new sustainable clothes. It's my life's mission to prove you can have your sustainable high-fashion cake and eat it."

The question is does this new environmentally friendly craze in the fashion industry have a basis in Judaism? The Torah (Bible) addressed this issue a long time ago with the commandment of bal tashchist, being a sin to waste or destroy. "Waste not" has long been a basic Jewish ethic involving the physical and spiritual worlds. Forbidding wasteful acts has a direct effect on our lives and our planet, each of which are G-d's creations.

The terrible sin of waste starts with G-d's specific instructions on destroying trees during wartime occupation. When laying siege to a city, we are commanded not to destroy fruit-bearing trees. "You must not destroy its trees. You may eat of them, but you must not cut them down. Are trees of the field to remove before you enter the besieged city? Only trees that you know do not yield food may be destroyed." Devorim (Deuteronomy 20:19-20). The general prohibition against needless destruction, derived from the verse Maimonides (Rambam) explains that a Jew is forbidden to "smash household goods, tear clothes, demolish a building, stop up a spring, or destroy articles of food." (Mishna Torah law of kings 6:10). Rabbi Samson Raphael Hirsch (1808–1888, Germany) explains in strong language that lo tashchit, "do not destroy," is "the most comprehensive warning to human beings not to misuse the position which G-d has given them as masters of the world and its matter through capricious, passionate, or merely thoughtless wasteful destruction of anything on earth."

I also explored a beautiful example of recycling from the Bais Hamikdash (Holy Temple). In the Mishnah (Tractate Sukkah 5:3) there is a description of Simchas Beis Hashoeva (celebration during The Feast of Weeks), a celebration in which tall menorot (candelabras) were lit that illuminated every courtyard in Jerusalem. The candlelight was so intense that a woman would have been able to see well enough to sort her wheat grains. The wicks for these flames were made from the worn-out garments of linen of the Kohanim (priests) who served in the Holy Temple.

A similar account is found in the Ten Plagues and their interesting and personal sensitivities. The plagues of blood and lice were given over to Aaron (Moses' elder brother) only. For Moses to have issued the plagues over the water and dust would have been highly disrespectful since the water protected him as an infant in the basket, and the dust helped him when he killed and buried the Egyptian slave master. Moses had a debt of gratitude and was beholden toward the dust and the water for their effect on his life. Rebbe Menachem Mendel of Kotzk learned an important lesson of gratitude from Moshe's backseat approach to the plagues of lice and blood.

It is obvious by the Torah's (Bible's) handling of waste that we learn how holy everything really is. From a fruit tree to a scrap of linen belonging to the Kohen, all aspects of respecting an object are clear. It might be too much to ask us to behave like Moses, who was indebted to the waters of the Nile and the earth particles of Egypt, to pay homage to the great earth that nourishes us. Understanding that each act of repurposing, recycling, or reimagining is really a sign of gratitude to Hashem (G-d) for creating and sustaining us.

The next time you toss your old shoes or finish your water bottle at the gym, or box up old clothes, remember to recycle them correctly because you might just be wearing it next season.

The Runway to the New Year

Fashion Week is held in February and September of each year and is a series of events (lasting 7–9 days) where international fashion collections are shown to buyers, the press, and the public. There are four major fashion weeks in the world, collectively known as the "Big 4", along with those in Paris, London, and Milan. The Council of Fashion Designers of America (CFDA) created the modern centralized "Fashion Week," starting in New York in 1993. NYFW, New York Fashion Week, is based on a much older series of events called "Press Week," founded in 1943.

I have been involved with New York Fashion Week since its creation by Fern Mallis under the tents of Bryant Park. I wish I had an entire book to tell you the backstage stories of my own personal accounts of the shows I have produced. From shutting down Central Park South at the peak of traffic to allow a ball gown collection to ride in the horse and carriages, to sponsoring an embroidery project with a group of talented ladies in the Negev Desert of Israel.

Funny episodes of hungry model breakdowns, makeup mood disorders, press re-releases, and wardrobe malfunctions. There are endless fittings, front row VIP approvals, celebrity handlers, designer egos, and body image issues which have since been humanized. You need to be a diplomat, healer, psychiatrist, agent, Indian chief and spiritual leader to successfully manage a real runway show. It looks much more glamorous than the hard work of a team of artisans who make it happen. It is like Cinderella, where the fairy godmother with a team of talented mice and birds put together her gown for the ball along with the pumpkin coach and horses.

Since the world has changed, fashion has certainly caught up. Tom Ford, chairman of The CFDA has changed the focus of New York Fashion Week to become more inclusive with the American Collections Calendar. Traditional fashion shows have now pivoted to keep up with the digital age through live streaming and other creative virtual outlets.

I think about how the enormous undertaking of the presentation of a major collection reminds me of the preparation for the High Holy Days. What could any Fashion Week have in common with the Rosh Hashanah (Jewish New Year), High Holiday season?

I asked this question to a team of industry experts. They are David and Nathanaelle Haines, founders of Fashion Week Studio who produce shows during Paris Fashion Week, Milan Fashion Week and have moved into live streaming shows from their studio location.

They drew a parallel between preparation for Fashion Week and their presentation to G-d. As G-d blessed them with opportunity to grow, they built an environment where a designer can grow. As G-d has given them a purpose, they have provided a space for the designer to fulfill his purpose.

Tobi, "Does fashion have any room for faith?"

David and Nathanaelle, "Fashion absolutely involves faith. We believe for any designer to muster up the courage to display the most intimate aspect of themselves to the world via their designs, requires much faith. To know that G-d has set within them a vision which will enlighten the world, bring about an abundance of happiness, and compliment and heighten another's self-image is the manifestation of faith indeed.

Tobi, "If a fashion show could compose a prayer what would it be?"

David and Nathanaelle, "It would acknowledge G-d and His blessings on everyone from the designers, to the models, to the photographers, to the hair and makeup team, to the sound and light crew, to the film crew, the producers, and the audience, to all happily share in the celebration of the aesthetic creations inspired by G-d, manifested through the designers and their purpose."

I want to explore the idea that it takes a village to help bring your best version to present to G-d. It takes an enormous amount of preparation to make it to the first of Tishrai, which is The Jewish New Year and the beginning of The High Holidays.

Repentance, potential and growth, are not self-contained projects. They need cooperation and work by people that surround you. At Fashion Week, where photographers, designers, models, handlers, film crews, sound, press, and audience all contribute to the purpose of the event, similarly an assortment of teams are needed for our presentation to G-d.

Rosh Hashanah is our big runway show, our Fashion Week.

Just as any well-planned show, it takes months of work. The process of T'shuvah (repentance and self-improvement) takes a village. The T'shuvah team consists of family, Rabbis, Rebbetzins, trusted friends, well selected confidants, mentors, lectures, videos, bible classes, and so much more. You may not realize how many components prepare our mind, body, and soul for the High Holiday version of our best selves.

This year and every year be thankful to the team of people that got you through to this point. Whether you have a fairy godmother and a pumpkin, stylist and coach, Rabbi and Rebbetzin or David and Nathanaelle Haines, they all helped prepare you to walk into your next Rosh Hashanah, the High Holiday Fashion Week of your life.

Tel Aviv Fashion Week

When you research Motty Reif, you immediately conclude that there is nothing he cannot do. Israel's answer to Simon Cowell, Tony Robbins, and Anna Wintour, all rolled up into the most famous, iconic, cultural figure in the Middle East. Motty Reif's Tel Aviv Fashion Week is a celebration of positivity with energy of love and acceptance.

Living in Israel, you can easily succumb to a myriad of divisive and negative issues such as elections, terror, peace, and world acceptance. However, he stays steadfast and true to who he is, an admirer, lifelong appreciator, nurturer, and sustainer of women. He views their true selves from the inside first and then the outside, as a complete beautiful canvas.

During Tel Aviv Fashion Week 2015, I was a guest of his production company and the bureau of Israel tourism/business council. At the time, Motty was producing a three-day fashion event in conjunction with the completion of a new Gindi-owned mega brand fashion mall in Tel Aviv. The number of shows, designers, models, makeup teams, hair teams, production crews, lighting crews, security, sponsors, and attendees was staggering, but Motty remained the cool major general of the fashion armies he commanded. I was so impressed, I tried to find a way to work with him in NYC.

We worked together with the Israeli Consulate (NYC) in 2016 with The Shankar School of Design. We managed to assemble the first fashion float in The Israel Day Parade with models and Israeli diplomatic figures. He could not be more gracious with his knowledge and enthusiasm. It was thrilling and a bit crazy.

Motty's Tel Aviv fashion week welcomes diversity. His modeling standards are spun around many sizes, ages, and races. "I believe that in the fashion industry there cannot be only one type of model," said Motty Reif to Vogue. "I have been working 33 years and I have been listening to women all my life saying, 'This is beautiful, but it isn't for me.' The fashion industry has a responsibility to change that. Imagine if fashion labels used models parallel to their clients?"

That is a very bold statement coming from the man that calls Bar Refaeli his BFF. Motty could adopt a haughty attitude with his movie productions, TV shows, photography exhibits, real estate consulting, and large lifestyle but he is surprisingly and unexpectedly humble.

When I first texted him my list of questions in 2019, he was knee deep in preparations for the upcoming TLV Fashion Week sponsored by Dove. How do you ask someone like this about G-d?

Tobi, "Do you think your talents are G-d given?"

Motty, "I believe that each of us come into this world with a purpose, being talented is part of your tools and role, you can improve it and use it to invent yourself with that G-d given gift."

Tobi, "How has your faith been incorporated into your work?"

Motty, "I believe that everything in my life, especially my work starts with faith. Diligence and hard work are the other important steps to succeed."

Tobi, "Has fashion become faithless, or is faith now fashionable? "

Motty, "I see fashion as not only clothing, but it is also our way we feel about ourselves. Fashion can be used to feel better about ourselves.

However, fashion today has more faith than ever. My work in celebrating women of all shapes and sizes is proof that fashion has grown up to include faith in oneself."

Tobi, "If your work could compose a prayer, what might that sound like?"

Motty, "My work has so many ways of beats, it is a long session of music that sounds like a brilliant symphony, a musical prayer."

Since then, life in Israel has been shut down, reopened, shut down and reopened again. All this would wreak havoc on anyone but Motty who seemed thrilled with his time at home. He has gotten more spiritual in his approach and outlook on life, women, and fashion. His social media posts on the Torah (Bible) portion of the week proves what I mean.

"On the Book of Names, a moment before a fashion week 2021 we were working. I was thinking about slavery in exterior appearance. Today's experience and desire to match the natural to a certain beauty ideal, an ideal imposed from the outside, that shows us exactly what a beautiful woman should look like. I say that this beauty ideal, and how much the effort there is to fulfill this ideal, is simply slavery."

Tobi, "What is the role of the fashion world in all this?"

Motty, "There is no doubt that the fashion world has a part in creating the situation, in that for years we have only shown models that meet very reduced criteria of weight, height, age range and so on."

TLV Fashion week continues with evolving the ideal of true beauty. Slavery to an outer beauty dictated by the industry that profits from it and societal standards has been going on for decades. Women have been trying to live up to these impossibilities since the printing press was invented. Motty means to take his show through an exodus, into the freedom of authenticity of the feminine form.

He has a surprisingly treasured humility despite the glamorous life he chose as his career path.

I read an article by the great Lord Rabbi Jonathan Saks where he mentions that "true humility is one of the most expansive and life-enhancing of all virtues. It does not mean undervaluing yourself. It means valuing other people. It signals a certain openness to life's grandeur and the willingness to be surprised, uplifted, by goodness wherever one finds it."

Motty found all that in the most unlikely places, the business of fashion.

Faux News

There was a time that a mink coat represented a higher social level. Sporting a floor-length sable was the ultimate in reaching the peak of a luxury lifestyle. A fur coat is wonderful winter accessory. It is hard to find a fashionable person not sporting a shiny down puff coat with a thick fur trimmed hood. Moncler, Canadian Goose or Moose Knuckles are tempting us with the coziness of warmth and swag. However, the mink covered moral compass of fashion has spun in another direction.

The House of Chanel took a bold step by banning fur and exotic skins from its collections. They officially announced they wanted to maintain ethical standards in their corporate framework. The internationally renowned French fashion house will stop producing garments and accessories made from animal fur, along with skins such as crocodile, lizard, and snake. The press release reads, "At Chanel, we are continually reviewing our supply chains to ensure they meet our expectations of integrity and traceability. In this context, it is our experience that it is becoming increasingly difficult to source exotic skins which match our ethical standards."

Versace, Gucci, Michael Kors, and Armani have also eliminated fur from their collections. Faux fabrications of sumptuous outerwear have become the new symbols of luxury and glamour.

The Giorgio Armani companies pronounced that, "Technological progress made over the years allows us to have valid alternatives at our disposal that render the use of cruel practices unnecessary in regard to animals".

In 2020, the state of Israel banned fur sales for the entire country. Environmental Protection Minister Gila Gamliel said the use of skin and fur for the fashion industry was "immoral." Her ministry said future permits would only be considered under certain, limited criteria which I guess might be about Shraimels (fur hat worn by some Chasidish men).

The big question is whether a real fur coat is halachically (Jewish law) permissible?

What does the Torah (Bible) teach us about the use of animals? I gaze at my adorable Wheaton Terrier, named Lady Cinnamon Babka, and think I may be the biggest hypocrite wearing a green fox trimmed puffer coat while I take her for walks each day. My Zaidy (grandfather) the late Michael Roth, impressed upon me how I must feed my dog before I eat myself based on one of the 613 Mitzvots. Is it incongruent that I fill her bowl with veterinarian-approved expensive dog food while I wear my Helen Yarmak grey sheered mink cardigan?

In Judaism, as in secular ethics, we find two distinct bases for this concern. Humane relations with animals are primarily governed by the prohibition on tza'ar baalei chaim, literally animal suffering. The basis of this prohibition is the belief that animals are worthy of ethical concern. They have feelings and a capacity for enjoyment or pain, even if not on a human level.

The Torah (Bible) says that man was given dominion over animals and permitted to use them for his needs. The beginning of Breishis (Genesis 1:26) instructs us that G-d gave man "dominion over the fish of the sea, and the birds of the air; the beasts, and the entire land; and all the creatures that creep on the land." Adam named all the creatures, showing his position of control (Genesis 2:20) and after the flood G-d promised Noah that the animals will be in awe of man's dominant position, and allows mankind to eat meat (Genesis 9:2-3).

But like all privileges in the Torah (Bible), this privilege is accompanied by responsibility of action and intent. The late Chief Rabbi of Tel Aviv, Rabbi Chayyim David Halevi, ethically deals with this topic in his volume of Responsa ("Mayim Chayyim", vol. 2, 1995).

He was approached by a protestor outside a cantorial concert who was disturbed by audience members wearing fur coats. The Rabbi was challenged by his question about why people would not choose to wear woolen garments instead of real fur if they wanted to dress well and warmly. Rabbi Halevi responded that though both man and the animals were created by G-d, man is the pinnacle of creation and has Divine sanction to use animals for his benefit.

Eating meat, which includes slaughtering animals, is permitted by the Torah (Bible), but hunting animals for the purpose of enjoyment or entertainment is not.

It is forbidden to kill animals painfully "in order to beautify and warm oneself with their skins." Some, but not all rabbis allow animals to be killed for the sake of their furs, but it must be done swiftly and without causing suffering to the animal. However, Rabbis are not supervising the mink farms. There are no mashgiachs tagging along on a fox hunt. Nor are there shomrim sporting a camouflage suit while shooting a lynx in the snow.

It is clearly better to use wool and the newest faux fur. Wool shearing and the new synthetics do not require the death of animals. Perhaps you can recycle your mother's fabulous mink coat without buying a new one. Sustainable uses of fur could range from shopping vintage stores to repurposing a coat you have already purchased or inherited.

Tomer Devorah by the Ramak, Rabbi Moshe Cordavaro, gives a deeper purpose for G-d's creatures and why they deserve human respect. Chapter 3,

18th of Month "...Supernatural chochmah (wisdom) reason, we are warned by our Sages against treating food disrespectfully." "For this reason, Rabbi Yehudah, "the Holy One" was punished, because he did not have pity on a calf that hid under his cloak, to evade slaughter, and he said to it, "Go! You were created for this purpose," (Bava Metzia 85a). Suffering, which derives from the aspect of strict judgement, came upon him. For only compassion shields against strict judgement. Thus, when he had mercy on a weasel, and said "His compassion is upon all His creations," (Tehillim 145:9), he was delivered from strict judgement, for the light of chochmah (wisdom) spread over him, and his suffering was removed."

"Similarly, one should not disparage any creature that exists, for all of them were (created) with chochmah (wisdom) nor should one uproot plants or kill animals unless they are needed."

"This is the general principle. Having pity not to ruin living creatures is contingent on chochmah (wisdom). Except when elevating them to a higher level, from plant to animal, or from animal to human, then it is permissible to uproot a plant or slaughter a live animal, causing damage to bring merit."

As mentioned by great and wise Nachmanides also known as The Ramban, in connection with the development of human character traits, the more we feel a sense of empathy toward animals, the more abusing them will heighten our sense of ethical sensitivity towards people as well. Let us be kind to animals and to one another.

Say Amen to the Dress

My daughter's paternal grandfather loved to share the story of all the shidduchim (marriage arrangements) that were made during those stressful yet liberating times after WW2. Displaced Persons Camps (DP Camps) for Jewish Holocaust survivors were established in Austria in 1945 by UNRRA (United Nations Relief and Rehabilitation Agency). They were administered by the U.S. Army and UNRRA and later by the International Refugee Organization (IRO). The camps existed until 1952. The number of Jewish residents in the camps was highest in 1948 when it reached 25,000. In this one, there was one precious wedding gown shared amongst the survivors temporarily residing there. Every wedding was a celebration of triumph over extinction with the exact same white wedding dress in attendance. As if it was a bold badge of honor passed from one bride to another with absolute faith in better days to come.

When reading Pearl Benisch's book, **Carry Me in Your Heart**, I was struck by a similar story. The book is a tribute to Sarah Schnerer, founder of The Bais Yaackov Movement. If I could have dinner with any person in the world, I would choose her for she is the epitome of courage, perseverance, tenacity, and truth. She is the most qualified role model for development of Jewish women's ever expanding brain power. The Bais Yaackov movement was a brain trust for the future of our survival.

The author addresses the subject of a particular dress in another DP Camp. Eda, a student of Sarah's, was gifted a dress for serving in the Bekleidungskammer, the apparel section of Bergen Belsen where all prisoners clothes were collected, curated, and documented, making certain that no such dignity remained on any Jew. However, a special dress was allotted to her, she altered it and gifted it to another woman who needed to be presentable for foreign dignitaries. Soon the same dress appeared on many girls dating boys with the intention to marry. The dress represented a renewed beauty and love.

Another "great dress," was worn as a bridal and festive dress by urban Spanish Jewish women who were descendants of the Jews expelled from Spain in 1492, in Morocco. The ensemble was designed with metal thread-embroidery as an ode to the Spanish costume of the sixteenth century. The dress became a visual symbol of the preservation of Spanish heritage.

"Collective Effort," the movie project, follows the creation of a special dress made from fabric hand-painted by Jewish families. The film traces the journey from the original sketch to the finished dress on a runway model. The final product is a testimony to creativity, endurance. and cooperation being sewn together by a special assortment of people through the means of faith and fashion. If that is not a dress after my own heart, what is?

Leonid Gurevich is the brain and talent behind this project and film. He is the fashion editor, stylist, photographer, producer, and more.

Leonid paid me the best compliment when I read his answers to my questions that were discussed this book. "I have learnt a great deal from you, Tobi, about the hidden messages in Judaism, and the connection between it and fashion, something I can't thank you enough for."

Tobi, "Are you able to see faith woven with fashion?"

Leonid, "I absolutely can see the connection between faith and fashion. Fashion is a serious business. And just like in any serious business, success is impossible without faith. Faith in your brand, faith in yourself, faith in your team, faith in the fact that success is a direct result of a hard, diligent work. In that sense, yes, I have utmost faith in it.

The abundance of creative inspiration coming directly from houses of worship into fashion collections, is undeniable. Also, faith and religion have been dictating dress codes throughout the centuries, which in turn influence what people wear. Look at the Hasidic community's style code, for instance, every aspect has strict rules from the length of the skirt to the shape of the wig.

When it comes to viewing the finished product and having nothing to do with what any artist had in mind, I am going to rephrase the famous saying and say, "the beauty is in the eye of the BELIEVER." Meaning that once an artist completes a project, there is no way to control how it is going to be judged, and if the viewer happens to be religious, then their perception will be influenced through the religious prism. I see it all the time. When a bird is singing, it may or may not sing about G-d, but to religious person, there is no doubt that it is praising the Lord.

The deeper I dove into the work on my "Collective Effort" film, sponsored by COJECO's (Council of Jewish Émigré Community Organizations in affiliation with the UJA Federation) Blueprint Fellowship program, the more I realized that despite the obvious differences, the world of Judaism and the world of Fashion have incredibly a lot in common.

Both worlds are full of mystery and hidden symbolism. Both require passionate devotion, perseverance, and utmost belief in the outcome. Both instill awe and fear in people unfamiliar with it. Both are often misunderstood by outsiders. And both are an endless source of inspiration.

I am trying to highlight these parallels in my film. I want people to see them as I see them, to experience and understand them, and most of all I would love people to enjoy them as I enjoy them.

Tobi, "Does your film and dress have a spiritual message?"

Leonid, "Absolutely. My film is precisely about a spiritual journey first with fashion coming second. You see, growing up as a Jewish kid in Russia, dealing with Anti-Semitism, being forced to leave the country you were born in, becoming an immigrant, a foreigner in another land, was not exactly what one would call a "cloudless childhood."

Even though Israel accepted us with open arms, we still had to work extremely hard to become proper citizens from learning the language to learning the ways of the new country. Then I had to repeat the entire process from scratch by coming to the US in my teens. Of course, it left a mark on my psyche, even though I never spoke about it publicly, until now, with "Collective Effort." The film is about finding and coming to terms with one's Jewish identity, with immigrant identity, and artistic identity. Anyone associating themselves with any of these categories will be able to relate and enjoy it.

The reason I am bringing the fashion aspect into this project, is because my profession just happens to be as a designer, stylist, and a fashion editor coming from the fashion world. As I am continuing to uncover my Jewish identity, I wanted to make that journey interesting and engaging for the Jewish community that may have never been exposed to the mysterious world of fashion. It is a cultural exchange of sorts. I came to learn about my Jewish culture, but I did not come empty handed. I am bringing a piece of my artistic universe with me and invite people to not just passively watch, but to actively participate.

The Dress that is being created in the movie is acting as a symbolic "Point of Merge" of the two worlds, both Spiritual and Physical, both Divine and Scientific, where all the participants bring their experiences to the table, creatively speaking."

Tobi, "Has your journey with your project brought you closer to your Judaism? If so, how?"

Leonid, "Oh, it absolutely did, and then some. The reason, I wanted to do this project with COJECO in the first place, was because I wanted to be closer to the Jewish community, closer to Jewish history and culture, to learn more about it and about myself as a part of it. It made me aware that I am not alone on my path. I have centuries worth of the DNA of my people in every molecule in my body. I made the 180 degree turn from someone who tried concealing his Jewish identity (which is understandable for someone who was bullied for it to the point of leaving his country of birth) to embracing it and being proud of it."

Never underestimate the power of the dress because it can be transformative. As in all these examples, the dress has a purpose of its own that is transmitted to the wearer. It is very personal because of the connection to memories and stories. It can be just a piece of cloth stitched together, but in these cases, it is a visual accomplice to a meaningful intention, strengthened by the time and reality in which it was worn. Can I get an AMEN to that?

When Hip Hop Was Jewish

In 2002, me and my fabulous partners, broke through the glass ceiling of Hip-Hop urban wear and launched our own brand, Ched-da, to Kmart as an exclusive collection. After being challenged by the big boys at Phat Farm, Sean John and Rocawear, we earned our place in the top 50 brands of streetwear. Although, it did not end well with revolving CEOs at Kmart, combined with limited production capabilities.

We were certainly crowned with street credibility and a lot of positive press, however, the best label I received was from my younger family members that admired my "cool factor."

In 2008, my 11-year-old cousin straight out of Bobov's domain in Boro Park was having a Jewish identity problem. He was "acting up" and wanted to change his name to a more secular version. He was also a big fan of rap/hip hop personalities and music. His parents were concerned and wanted to turn him around to a better place.

At my suggestion, he spent a good portion of that summer with me. I hoped I could influence him with my scheme to renew his Jewish pride. Since I had his trust because I was "cool," I defined my rules: if he behaved himself all summer, he would collect points he could use to meet the biggest celebrity rap star in the world (at the time). Having no idea who it was, he was great all summer, staying at the synagogue on Shabbos, talking respectfully and listening to me. I was impressed.

Little did he know, my friend Seth Gerszberg and his partner Marc Ecko owned the most important urban brand at the time called "Ecko Unltd" with hundreds of millions in sales. They operated out of a renovated 275,000-square-foot headquarters on West 23rd St. They also owned "G-Unit by 50 Cent," hip hop's biggest personality. I called Seth and told him my cousin's story about his lack of interest in yeshiva and Jewish practices. We came up with the ultimate plan to effect change in my house guest. Of course, I clued in his mom and dad and they were excited for his upcoming experience.

At the end of that summer, I took my little cousin and his mom to Ecko headquarters. We were greeted by the giant rhino mascot, and escorted upstairs to the showroom where we were surrounded by the largest stocked candy store. Our eyes were overcome by the art, furniture and display cases that were so creatively engaging. Seth Gerszberg, sporting a Breslov white yarmulke, came out to welcome us to Ecko land. Naturally, the boy was shocked and impressed that the owner of this place was Jewish and religious.

Seth introduced his sales staff that were terribly proud to have been recruited from Gush Katif, Israel, right after the horrendous surrender to the PLO. Seth generously gave my cousin some branded clothing along with a grand tour, which included a full basketball court. It was a boy's fantasy, but the best part was yet to come. As we viewed each incredible floor, we finally got to G-Unit, and you would think we landed in a diamond mine. Two muscular bodyguards led us to a blinged out showroom. Just as we started to sit down, 50 Cent came out and said, "where is that boy that doesn't want to stay in yeshiva," and finished that sentence with his proper Hebrew name. I thought I might need to catch a fainting little boy and an awe-struck mom, but 50 Cent knew exactly what to do. He took out one of his bestselling hoodies and autographed it for him with the same words. 50 Cent and Seth Gerszberg turned this boy's world around. Not only did they customize a "kiruv" intervention, but they led by example. Never again did my cousin feel ashamed, challenged, or stigmatized by his schooling, neighborhood, name, or religion.

Yesterday I called my cousin, now a grown and accomplished man, to discuss the level of antisemitism within the hip-hop community. At the time Nick Cannon was saying stupid things on his podcast that ended his Wild 'N Out career with Viacom. 50 Cent received flak from others within his community that felt he should have been more supportive of Cannon and ignored his blatant anti-Jewish remarks. Thankfully, with outreach from

Morton Klein and others, positive movement has occurred to re-educate the falsities of hatred. Don't we have enough common ground to unite peacefully and harmoniously? I know for certain that we do.

Whatever went sour within the relationship between hip hop culture and Jews, we are incredibly happy that over 170 US celebrities joined the Black Jewish Alliance with the intention of strengthening the relationship between the black and Jewish communities with the power of the entertainment community. Celebrities like Tiffany Haddish, Nick Canon, Gene Simmons and Mayim Bialik are among the assortment of A-list celebrities involved in this important initiative.

My family will always praise and continue to reminisce about 50 Cent, and Seth and his wonderful company. We will cherish and never forget the story of one little yeshiva boy from Boro Park that learned to be a proud Jew from a Hip-Hop Rap Star.

What to Wear When Moshiach Arrives

At first, I thought this would be a comical question to ask a few friends. After all, I have been quarantined for too long, plus recuperating from surgery. If you are a social person like me, you know that the lack of outside entertainment such as parties, weddings and other events can make you stir crazy. Since I continuously inform my husband that Moshiach (Messiah) is coming any minute now, I thought I should use this time to decide what to wear for the most momentous occasion of a lifetime.

Going through my closets, I gravitated towards the ballgowns that danced me through the wonderful highlights of my life. Of course, I chose my favorite Carolina Herrera white jersey gown with jet black beaded flowers placed all over the front panels. After all, this is the most important and life changing event of all time. Maybe it was the pain meds that were responsible for this crazy fashion exercise, but the selection started to confirm its reality.

Thinking that I simply cannot be the only one doing this, I called a few friends to see if I was alone in my wardrobe planning. To my delightful surprise, every woman that I contacted had an outfit preselected for Moshiach's entrance.

Estee Goldschmidt, founder of Shop Drop, has a two-season solution to the big fashion question. "It depends on if Moshiach coming in the winter or the summer. If summer, I will pair my Alexander Wang heeled sandals with an ivory Badgley Mischka twist dress. If winter, I am wearing a Lela Rose sweater with a blazer (Russian style). For the bottom, my Réalisation silk midi skirt paired with J. Campbell pointed heeled sock boots." Since she is the daughter of Pinchas Goldschmidt, Chief Rabbi of Moscow, Russia, and President of The Conference of European Rabbis, she knows a thing or two about Moshiach's importance.

Hillary Barr, CEO of R New York Real Estate, immediately texted me back with a definite "Outfit picked out and bags packed. White eyelet dress down to my ankles." My vivacious childhood friend and event planner, Altchie Pelcowitz, messaged me, "I should say white. But knowing me, I chose a black Valentino."

Galit Udel Winer, founder of Kidichic childrenswear thought deeply about it. "Something white. Something fun from my collection. I'm thinking something with a stunning lace collar that will work perfectly to fly on the wings of Moshiach."

Rebbitzen Malka Werde, Director of Chabad at FIT included her best sheitel (wig) with her outfit. "My favorite Sheitel #1. My finest jewelry, and my one-piece patterned dress from Tzefas."

"A white midi dress with gold thread in the shape of a flower. Something super pure and shiny," is the outfit for Ahuva Levy, co-founder of Shop Drop.

Fashion

This wild question meant only to entertain, has taken on a life of its own. If you dig deeper, past the seemingly frivolous notion of the attire, you will see the neon bright lights of pure Emunah (faith) and complete joy in anticipation of Moshiach. This is where you find the housing of the Shechinah (glory) that rests in every Jewish woman's soul.

The Lubavitcher Rebbe describes it best. "The righteous women are (essentially) imbued with the feeling of joy; a joy so great that it is expressed in song, because of the greatness of the trust that, behold he (Moshiach) is coming, and he has already come!" (Jan 6, 1992)

Our sages tell us that "in the merit of righteous women our ancestors were redeemed from Egypt." It was the women who never despaired during G-d's redemption possessing unwavering trust in His process.

The Midrash explains that the Jewish women, while still in Egypt, were so confident that they would be redeemed, that they prepared tambourines for the day when they would sing a song of gratitude with Miriam leading the procession.

The Arizal explains the Kabbalistic connection as the souls of the final generation before Moshiach's arrival are reincarnations of the souls of the generation of the Exodus. Repeating the reality of meriting the Jewish woman with the survival of the Jewish nation for generations.

Once again it will be the women of our generation, with their unshakeable belief in the Redemption, that will escort in the Moshiach.

Naturally, I must ask ladies, what are you planning to wear?

The Passover Collection

As a child, my mother started shopping for my Passover wardrobe immediately following Purim. The spree began with excursions to Williamsburg, Boro Park, Union Turnpike, including the beloved Alexander's and Ohrbach's. I despised dressing up and every trip to the fitting room was a nightmare. I hated the poof, the twirl, and the bows as much as the ruffle ankle socks and patent leather shoes. However, it was an unwritten law that a brand-new wardrobe was a "must" for the Passover season.

As you can safely guess, I grew out of my disgust for fashion and grew into my complete adoration for it. I took this "Passover wardrobe renewal" concept theory to the next retail level. I am guilty of overindulgence with every program I attended starting from the Crown Hotel in Miami during the 80's to the Biltmore in Coral Gables. If you are styling your wardrobe options for the United Arab Emirates getaway adventure of a lifetime or coordinating outfits for your Seder at the family table, Passover is more than just matzah. Maybe they should add a line in the Haggadah to include "pesach, matzah, marror and clothes." I am only joking.

Where did this obsession start? How can a holiday based on freedom enslave you with wardrobe selection? Seems a juxtaposition of gashmius vs ruchniyis (spirituality vs. materialism). It is a custom amongst Chassidim to adorn your wife with new clothes and jewelry for every Yom Tov. I called Rav Moshe Vorhand of The Heichel Moshe Vorhand shul (synagogue) on the Upper West side of Manhattan, to get the scoop and Torah (Bible) source on this wonderful tradition.

Rav Moshe Vorhand shared, "The custom to buy new clothing for Yom Tov is in the Ramban (rabbeinu Rav moshe Ben maimon) hilchos Yom Tov (chapter 6, Halacha 17). "A person is obligated to be happy in them (the days of Yom Tov) and in good spirit together with his children and his wife and grandchildren, etc. as it is written "v'samachta b'chagecha" etc. even though included in that joy is to rejoice with his family accordingly.

How does one rejoice? To the children one gives delicacies, and the women one buys clothing and nice jewelry according to his ability. Men eat meat (steak) and wine and when one eats and drinks, he is obligated to give to the poor and indigent, and low spirit, etc." The Ramban's wisdom has great depth that touches each member of the family during the Holiday season that is tailor made to evoke absolute joy.

Fashion has a different twist for the man during this time. It is customary that the leader of the Seder (special meal) wears a plain white garment, or kittel while reclining on a pillow. According to the Chabad teaching, some reasons for this holiday attire are that the kittel resembles a burial shroud and thus serves to remind one of the futilities of vanity and pride in one's lifetime.

Others interpret this quite differently as the white garment reminds us of the white garments that the Kohen Gadol (high priest) would wear when he entered the Holy of Holies (inner chamber) while serving in the Bet HaMikdash (Holy temple). On this night of Passover, every Jew who leads the Seder service is like the Kohen Gadol's performance. It can also resemble a groom that declares his divine love for Hashem (G-d) for saving us from brutal slavery and starting us in a new path of Torah (Bible).

Before you get dressed in new clothes and jeweled accessories for your Seder in Queens, Brooklyn, Mexico, Spain, Italy, Abu Dhabi, Dubai, or Israel, meditate on the concept of attire being more just an outfit to wear. You are going to the Seder table with powerful wisdom from the Torah (Bible), Ramban and many more.

Lot's Wife Is a Muse

Maskit is Israel's first fashion house with a history of the country weaved into its fabric. Created in 1954 by Ruth Dayan, Moshe Dayan's wife (who recently passed away),, Maskit's genesis was to become a contemporary luxury clothing brand highlighting the traditional embroidery of its new immigrants. Maskit has graced iconic leading ladies such as Audrey Hepburn through collaborations with Dior and Yves Saint Laurent. The brand was dormant for a time. In 2013-2014 Sharon and Nir Tal relaunched the brand with the blessing of Ruth Dayan and her partners, Lynn, and Stef Wertheimer.

Sharon Tal was previously the embroidery director at Alexander McQueen before revitalizing Maskit. Her talent and experience paid tribute to the Maskit's past and forges its relevance into the future Israel's fashion houses.

In September of 2018, together with Eyal Nevo, one of the country's leading fashion photographers, they created a haunting campaign titled "Mount Sodom". Eyal Nevo is best known for his editorial and brand work. His creativity has appeared in Condé Nast Traveler, ELLE, and Marie Claire. He has orchestrated campaigns for major Israeli brands and collaborates Israel's top, and original, super model Bar Rafaeli.

The exhibition was during New York Fashion week. The collection featured a short film and photo exhibit. "Mount Sodom is inspired by the myths of the ancient city of Sodom and the contradictions of a land that at once both attracts and repels with the silence and violence of its landscape, magical presence of biblical history, and forceful aesthetics of industrialization." This is the explanation for the title of this presentation according to the press release of its sponsor ZAZIOTS.

Sharon Tal recounts, "Discussions about the ancient story of Sodom provoked emotions and images of once-magnificent landscapes, now degraded by industrialization. Together with 35 artists, we created a new and thought-provoking work that merges fashion and art." There is one particular photograph of Lot's wife looking distraught that struck me to the core and stayed embedded in my mind."

I recently asked Sharon about the ever-changing terrain of fashion and its duality of faith.

Tobi, "Has fashion become faithless?" She replied, "In some areas it has, but there are always the designers which you can tell by their collection that they are working from within their faith."

How can a depraved city like Sodom provoke beauty? Can Lot's wife be a fashion muse?

We all know the story of Sodom and Gomorrah, Lot, his wife, and the pillar of salt. Frankly, I never paid much attention to this woman until now. Initially, the concept repelled me into a rather judgmental critic. However, this unique presentation spurred such conflicted emotions in me that I had to learn more of her from the Torah (Bible) and other sources. The Torah (Bible) does not mention her Lot by name, but the Rabbis referred to her as "Idit" (Tanhuma [ed. Buber], Vayera 8).

This woman's demise teaches about her life. Even though she was rescued from the destruction of Sodom, she was stricken along with all inhabitants of the city. That implies she was no different than anyone living there at the time.

Sodom was a magnificent city with a disgusting core. Jealousy, moral deficiency, sexual depravity, and zero hospitality were its principles. When G-d sent his angels, they did not initially want to be Lot's wife's guests, but guest of her husband, since he was more righteous (Num. Rabbah 10:5). She tried to block their entry to the house. Lot's wife divided their house into two parts and told her husband, "If you want to receive them, do so in your part," (Gen. Rabbah 50:6). That was a" War of The Roses" way of running a household.

Lot wished to be hospitable by asking his wife to bring them salt. She responded, "Do you even wish to learn this bad habit from Abraham?" (Gen. Rabbah 50:4). She obeyed her husband's request, then plotted to remove the guests from her house by asking neighbors to borrow salt. They asked her, "Why do you need salt, why didn't you prepare enough beforehand?" She answered, "I took enough for our own needs, but guests came to us and it is for them that I need salt."

With this salt situation going "viral" all of Sodom knew that Lot was harboring guests. They stormed the front of his house and demanded that he hand them over to the townspeople. There is no logic to Lot's handling of the situation. He did so by offering his daughters to be gang raped as a compromise.

(Midrash Aggadah [ed. Buber], Gen. 19:26), "Because she sinned through salt, Lot's wife was punished by being turned into a pillar of the same material," (Gen. Rabbah 51:5).

The pillar of salt was left by G-d as a memorial (Yalkut Shimoni on Esth., para. 1056). Moses saw the pillar of salt that had been Lot's wife when G-d showed him the land of Canaan before his death.

Anyone who views Lot's wife is required to recite two brachot. First, "Blessed be the one who remembers the righteous," expresses thanksgiving and praise to G-d for having remembered Abraham, by zachus merit of whose righteousness G-d spared Lot and his wife from the destruction. The second is "Blessed be the true Judge." This is recited upon hearing of someone's death in memory of punishment visited on Lot's wife (BT Berakhot 54a–b).

Midrash Agadah relates that Lot's wife stands in her place to the present and everyday passing oxen lick her feet and every morning she rises again to her previous shape as a pillar of salt (Sefer ha-Yasha).

This time fashion and faith might collide not collaborate. Or is there always good that follows such evil?

Hashem (G-d) could have ended her life in any way, by changing her, or covering her in any substance. Yet Genesis tells us specifically that she became a pillar of salt. To the modern ear salt is a tasty element, but for thousands of years the primary function of salt was not as a seasoning but as a preservative. Is this an apt metaphor for Lot's wife? Is she preserved to teach us a lesson?

This leads to a new question. Is she a message of warning or a monument? We all have a version of her inside of us navigating a complicated dance between past nostalgia and future potential. Even if the past was horrible, abusive, or sinful we can get stuck looking back longingly. In cases of good or bad, we should be moving forward, not risking turning into a pillar of the past. Lot's wife teaches us the lesson of forward movement and divine forgiveness, even in cases where it is not deserved. Hashem (G-d) wants us to look forward to better futures in the Torah (Bible) rather than becoming stuck in our past.

Maskit with Sharon Tal at the helm, brings a revised meaning to the term fashion forward. Rather than being a fashion victim to the past, we all must move ahead with a new ensemble. Never to look back at the styles that did not suit us well. Sharon has respected the history of the label, yet she has masterfully marched onward.

Walk in My Shoes

I must confess that my own spiritual journey began with a pair of hot pink snakeskin Manolo Blahnik sandals. My brand "The House of Faith and Fashion," was born from the reality that women were often more interested in my Manolos than my religious practices. I decided that if I could combine the two, while teaching Judaic principles (Judaic knowledge), I would achieve a unique way to combine the world of spirituality and materialism, ruchnuis and gashmius.

In truth, my rebellious and flamboyant shoe selections came to life during high school in Queens, NY, with a pair of red cowboy boots. Bais Yackov of Queens (all girls religious school) during those years was not as stringent with dress codes as they are now. Although the length of our skirts was important, the rest was left up to us to nurture our own individuality.

I finally have my daughter join me in this. I am embarrassed to say that I started to cry when she tried on my hot pink satin bejeweled pumps as if I was reliving her Bat Mitzvah where she wore Manolo embroidered flats.

Manolo Blahnik's stilettos shot to fame after the premiere of HBO's 'Sex and the City' in 1998. Carrie Bradshaw, played by Sarah Jessica Parker, frequently professed her love for this shoe brand which included the famous sky-blue satin pair (Hangisi Satin 70mm pumps) that she wore when she finally married her Mr. Big. When I married my Mr. Wonderful, I wore a pair of the white lace version of the Hangisi Manola Blahniks.

Everyone these days seems to have an addiction. My addiction is shoes. Thank G-d there are no rehabs for that yet. I did shed a tear when the Manolo Blahnik flagship boutique on W 54th Street closed. The small shop was a temple of divine shoes, a magical kingdom for a shoe obsessed female. Currently, my vice has widened to Sarah Palmer from Australia, whose handmade footwear has graced the covers of Hong Kong and Qatar Harper's Bazaar. I am also craving a pair of clear lucid beauties from Amina Mauddy that are constantly waitlisted.

To satisfy my habits, I ask question, what does a pair of shoes have to do with the Torah (Bible)? One can say it is for Shalom Bayis, peace in the marital home as Manolo Blahnik once said, "Men tell me that I've saved their marriages. It costs them a fortune in shoes, but it is cheaper than a divorce. So, I am still useful, you see." Of course, the Torah (Bible) has a more meaningful approach to shoes with plenty of examples.

The Torah (Bible) depicts shoes as signs of sensuousness, comfort, and pleasure with a strong emphasis on when and where. Let us start with "According to the Code of Jewish Law" (the Shulchan Aruch), the detailed instructions for putting on shoes. The right shoe goes on first. When tying shoes, the left shoe is tied first. When shoes are taken off, the left shoe comes off first. This is based on the right being more important than the left. The right foot should not remain uncovered while the left is covered, a display of respect and modesty for the feet. Shoes should be tied from the left since knotted teffilin is worn on the left arm so that the tying of shoes replicates the tying of teffilin. During the Sholosh Regalim, when the priestly blessing is given by the Kohanim, they must remove their shoes outside the sanctuary before their hands are washed by the Levites; a minhag (custom) amongst certain Chassidic groups to remove their (leather) shoes before visiting a Tzadik's gravesite.

This was derived from the command Hashem (G-d) made to Moshe (Moses) when he approached the Burning Bush (Exodus 3:5), "Remove your shoes from your feet, for the place on which you stand is holy ground." On the saddest day of the year, Tisha b'Av, Jews are prohibited from wearing leather shoes. The same prohibition applies on Yom Kippur. Chalitzah, a rather interesting and rare ceremony in which the brother of the deceased can choose to release his sister-in-law to marry someone else. The widow and her brother-in-law both appear before a rabbinical court, a beth din, consisting of five members. The brother-in-law wears on his right foot a halitzah shoe. This special shoe is made from the skin of a kosher animal and consists of two pieces sown together with leather straps. It must not contain metal and is designed like a moccasin with long straps.

I remember when my father had to perform this ceremony with my aunt. In the Megillah of Ruth, Naomi cleverly instructs her daughter-in-law, Ruth, in the rules of seduction with her instruction to visit Boaz at night and uncover his feet. The Song of Songs 7:2 reads, "How beautiful are thy feet in sandals" lovingly written by King Solomon. The Talmud's dream interpretation lists various dreams that signal negative portents. One of them is if you dream of a dead person coming back and removing your shoes. Such a vision, says the Talmud, is bad news, with a sure visit by the Malach Hamaves, the angel of Death. Malachi's, angels are described as being barefoot. The absence of shoes represents the shedding of the body and identification with the soul. The Kohen Gadol ornately dressed are instructed to walk barefoot in order to remind him that his holy presence is deeply rooted in the ground.

In Rabbi Joseph B. Soloveitchik's "Blessing and Thanksgiving," he suggests that the enjoyment of a shoe is not the shoe itself, it is a social prestige. There is no special blessing for putting on a shoe, it is included in one big total blessing. The blessing is "who has provided all my need for me?" The shoe is important, but it does not have a special blessing for it.

Shoes in Jewish history have grown to haunt us. During my visit to Poland in 1990, I was struck and horrified by the endless piles of shoes in Auschwitz (concentration camp). Every holocaust museum has an exhibit of piles of shoes from children and adults. The Nazis removed the shoes as a sign of humiliation, despair, and certain death. Leaving the shoes to symbolize the paths that were taken and the road that will never be walked again.

"I have always believed that a beautiful shoe is useless unless it feels as wonderful as it looks," says Stuart Weitzman, founder of Stuart Weitzman Shoes. Shoe shopping can be elevated to include the dressing of a princess or queen.

I asked Sarah Palmer if she thought women worship shoes. Sarah answered. "I believe women do indeed worship shoes. No doubt many of us share in childhood memories of seeing our mother looking glamorous stepping into a pair of high heels. Stunning high heel shoes are worshiped by little girls who wish to be grown up enough to wear them."

I also believe that a shoe can transform a person, after all look how well Cinderella and Dorothy did with theirs. We are Hashem's (G-d's) princesses, and don't princesses need shoes?

This essay is dedicated to my papa Leonard Goldberg who I am honored to consider my second dad. He was the pioneer of discount designer shoe shops who owned "Pick A Shoe," throughout Florida. He reveled in my shoe shopping and scolded me for paying more than $28 a pair.. I adored his sense of humor and his remarkable talent. I thank him for teaching me the meaning of family with unconditional love and unwavering support.

Photo courtesy of Eyal Assulin

Fashion

Photo courtesy of Eyal Assulin

The House of Faith and Fashion

Photo courtesy of Kate McGuire, Converted Closet

Fashion

Photo courtesy of Fashion Week Studio

Photo courtesy of Fashion Week Studio

Fashion

Photo courtesy of Motty Reif

Photo courtesy of Motty Reif

Fashion

Photo courtesy of Motty Reif

Photo courtesy of Motty Reif

Fashion

Tobi Rubinstein

Maskit by Sharon Tal

Fashion

Photo by Tobi Rubinstein

Sarah Palmer Shoes by Abi Green

Sarah Palmer Shoes by Abi Green

The House of Faith and Fashion

Ched-da photo courtesy of Tobi Rubinstein

Fashion

NYFW with New York Horse and Carriages

The House of Faith and Fashion

CHAPTER 2

JEWELRY

"I adorned you with ornaments, put bracelets on your hands and a necklace around your neck. I also put a ring in your nostril, earrings in your ears and a beautiful crown on your head."
Ezekiel 16:11 12

Jewelry

Necklace by Tobi Rubinstein

Evil Eyed

Eyeballing the A-list celebrity jeweler, Lorraine Schwartz's "ayin harah" (evil eye) tennis bracelet, with perfectly matched diamonds, in the windows of The Badrutt Palace Hotel, St Moritz, will make any woman drool. Evil eye jewelry is being peddled at every price from luxury to street vendors. The Kabbalah Centers sell these spiritual adornments including the famous "red string" to their thousands of followers.

One cannot go to the Kotel (Western Wall) without being approached by numerous merchants that want to entice your spiritual awareness with special red strings. I googled "evil eye jewelry" and explored the hundreds of sites selling everything from amulets to ankle bracelets, toe rings to diamond rings, all boasting a metaphysical meaning.

The eye crosses over many religions and offers protection against so called negative energy. The red string is a boundary that keeps the positive forces in and the opposite out. I remember the delightful store on Main Street in Kew Gardens Hills called PEREG. Tucked between the scented spice barrels, assorted dried couscous mixes and etrog jelly, there was a mysterious shelf of anti-evil remedies such as preserved fisheyes and other "Shakespearian" ingredients. This reminded me of the witch's potion from childhood fables.

I had a very superstitious great grandmother and grandmother that used spitting three times to ward away any manifestations of the harmful eye. As a little girl I found the behavior a bit frightening. Every greeting came with a hug. kiss and spit. My great grandmother had issues with black jewelry and baths after Shabbos. I have no idea where these superstitions came from.

What are the origins of this jewelry trend? Does the Torah (Bible) mention anything about evil eyes and red strings, eye of Newt, black cauldrons or spitting?

Let us start with my favorite guide to practical life, Pirkai Avot (Ethics of The Fathers). In chapter two, the evil eye is discussed. Rabban Yohanan, "He said unto them, go forth and observe which is the right way to which a man should cleave. Rabbi Eliezer said, "A good eye." Rabbi Joshua said, "A good companion." Rabbi Yose said, "A good neighbor." Rabbi Shimon said, "Foresight." Rabbi Elazar said, "A good heart." Rabban Yohanan said, "To them I prefer the words of Elazar ben Arach, for in his words your words are included." Rabban Yohanan said, "Unto them, go forth and observe which is the evil way which a man should shun." Rabbi Eliezer said, "An evil eye."

In several pieces of Midrash, Rabbis suggest that the evil eye played a role in various incidents in the Torah (Bible). For example, Sarah cast an evil eye on Hagar while Hagar was pregnant, causing her to miscarry before a later pregnancy with Ishmael. Rabbis argue that Leah's fertility was adversely impacted when she "became subject to the power of the evil eye," for thanking G-d for allowing her to bear more than a fourth of Jacob's sons (Rabbeinu Bahya, Bereshit 30:38:5). In the Talmud, Rabbis say that Joseph's descendants are immune to the power of the Evil Eye, and that "One who enters a city and fears the evil eye should hold the thumb of his right hand in his left hand and the thumb of his left hand in his right hand and recite the following, I _____, son of _____, come from the descendants of Joseph, over whom the evil eye has no dominion." (Berakhot 55b)

In Mishnah Berurah, Jews are urged to perform the Rosh Hashanah Tashlich ritual in a body of water that contains fish because, "fish are incapable of being affected by the evil eye."

In an article from Torah.org by David Twersky, "The Chidah believes that a person with humility can escape the Evil Eye. Someone who is humble does not prance around and try to attract attention to himself. It is specifically such attention-grabbing actions that attract the Evil Eye." The Gematria of Ayin is 120, that of Anavah is 121. Thus, the Chidah says that one with Anivus "is above" the (Evil) Eye."

There is an entire book dedicated to all aspects or renditions of Eiyen Harah, intentionally or unintentionally fueled by jealousy or amazement (Sefer Ayin Hara by R' Moshe Yagudyov).

There are countless segulahs (amulets) discussed in the seforim (books) and it is beyond the scope of this essay to cite them. Ranging from a pregnant woman wearing the "even tekuma," a type of ruby, to prevent her from miscarrying, to direct prayers.

It is important to understand that segulahs of every variety work just like all other human endeavors, because ultimately everything is up to Hashem (G-d). If Hashem (G-d) does not desire something to happen, all the segulahs in the world will not help. If Hashem (G-d) wants something to happen, He sends the means to achieve His will which is not by man's segulah.

So, if your red string fell off in the shower, or your evil eye necklace that was a gift from your aunt in Tzfat suddenly broke, or if you cannot afford the Lorraine Schwartz diamond eye bracelet, do not have an anxiety attack over their power of protection over you. In all fairness, these pieces of jewelry probably attract more attention than they were ever intended to, almost achieving a reverse reaction. The only true protection we have is G-d Himself, but a few "k'nein a harahs" could not hurt!

The Jewels of Joy

"Life is big, and I like my jewelry even bigger!" This the perfect introductory quote from Liat Ginzberg, Israel's trendiest jewelry designer. We first connected years ago at Bijoux at The Norton Museum of ART. Since I am a big jewelry fan in every sense of the word, I immediately gravitated to Liat's collection. Over the years we formed a great friendship, and she has customized an assortment of pieces for me that are bold, beautiful, and brazen. They are perfectly suited for occasions like New York Fashion Week's runway shows and media appearances.

Liat has grown over the years to include a multitude of **Vogue** editorials, **L'eisha** and **Grazia,** plus the Israeli singing sensation NETTA wears her pieces. She has an A-List of collectors who value the category of Art Jewelry.

Liat Ginzberg's jewelry designs are daring, one-of-a-kind pieces, with her abundant use of color and electrifying style. The designs express a nostalgic yet current view on the 90's club scene combined with hints of Frida Kahlo, Carmen Miranda, Lucille Ball and Madonna.

Each piece is a composition of vintage pieces from the 70's and the 80's, which Liat collects around the world. All these elements and influences produce a unique style that is her own. Liat never capitulates to trends, she remains herself in each earring, bracelet, and necklace. Her designs will never fade to fads.

When I last saw Liat in Palm Beach, FL, I engaged her in an unlikely spiritual discussion she was not accustomed to. She is frequently interviewed by fashion magazines that focus only on her jewelry and how it relates to the subject of the moment. I wanted to explore her rather than her designs.

Tobi, "Do you think your talent is G-d given?"

Liat, "I was born with it. Along with my imagination developing in childhood."

Tobi, "Do you need faith in yourself to develop such unique jewelry?"

Liat, "Faith in yourself yes, it's all a part of me. It is my purpose; it is me and it is my calling that makes me. It is my essence that completes me. A singer sings. A writer writes. It is a gift with a cost, but it is worth it. It is a heavenly gift. I am not religious at all, but my gift is from above. This is me."

Tobi, "Do you believe that fashion can become someone's faith?"

Liat, "People put too much faith in their fashion. A person can become a victim of fashion. It never was like this for me, it comes naturally to me. The fashion jewelry that I create is a part of my being."

Tobi, "If your jewelry could compose a prayer, what might that look like?"

Liat, "It would be wonderful for people to have the joy of life.

Shimchat Chiam and Kidushat Chiam. My jewelry reflects the joy of life. Some people have everything but sadly they lack joy and gratitude for life. My jewelry reflects the happiness of life which one should have, one must have, to be fulfilled and healthy."

The state of happiness is a crucial part of life that G-d wants us to experience. Happiness is a Torah (Bible), Halacha, Chassidic, psychological, universal method to living a healthy, productive, and purposeful life. I could write another piece about the importance of happiness in Judaism. The month of Adar is the time we are commanded to celebrate in simcha (rejoicing).

"All these curses will befall you, pursuing you and overtaking you to destroy you because you did not obey the Lord, because you did not serve G-d, your G-d, with joy and gladness of the heart." Deuteronomy/Devorim 28:45, 28:47.

"Just as it is with a victory over a physical opponent, for instance two people who wrestle with each other, each striving to fell the other, if one of them is lazy and sluggish he will easily be defeated and will fall, even if he be stronger than the other--so it is with the conquest of one's evil nature: it is impossible to conquer the evil nature with laziness and sluggishness, which stem from sadness and a stone-like dullness of the heart, but rather with alacrity, which derives from joy and an open heart that is unblemished by any trace of worry and sadness in the world,"

Rabbi Schneur Zalman of Liadi, Tanya, Chapter 26 (34).

As taught by Rabbi Yaakov Klein, founder of the Lost Princess Initiative, the concept of simcha is an important one in Jewish philosophy. A popular teaching by Rabbi Nachman of Breslov, a 19th-century Chassidic Rabbi, is "Mitzvah Gedolah Le'hiyot Besimcha Tamid, "It is a great mitzvah (commandment) to always be in a state of happiness. When a person is happy, he is more capable of serving G-d and going about his daily activities than when depressed or upset."

Liat's unique style spreads her light, love, and sparkle through the happiness she injects into every piece of jewelry she makes. She is hoping to transfer her "simcha" to the women who wears her designs. What a joyful way to get blinged.

Guard Your Lips

I was in awe of Keren Wolf's jewelry the moment she presented her accessories for the Matan Shakan Collection, Negev themed runway show. Face masks of golden roses were combined with dresses of nude colored tulle, and sequins adorned the models. Her pieces were visions of beauty that left the audience and press speechless.

It is no surprise that her work graces the covers of top fashion publications like "Elle's" recent issue with Cardi B. Madonna, Lady Gaga, Kylie Jenner, Chrissy Teigen, and Lana Delray can be found wearing her designs on their tours, in videos, and editorials. Her Instagram page is star studded. She is a former top actress herself with a keen understanding of what stars want.

Great respect should be given to her as she describes her art installation and collection with a sentence from scripture. "It is said that death and life are in the power of the tongue (Proverbs 18:21), a concept so powerful, that it inspired me to design and create the "Big Mouth" collection."

"The collection is built around the notion that words can be used to inspire, to influence, and to create, at the same time they can be used to destroy and oppress." Those are deep and powerful words all rooted in the Torah (Bible).

The power of speech is expressed in many ways. The most elevated way is through song. When a person is filled with strength, speaking alone is not always enough. An example was during the Jewish exodus from Egypt and the miraculous crossing of the Reed Sea. Words alone could not express their gratitude to G-d, therefore they had to sing.

Maybe that explains why I want to break out into a song every time I see another Instagram post on Keren Wolf's page.

Getting in touch with Keren about her faith was where I started, then I learned a lot more about her.

Tobi, "Do you believe that your talent is a gift from G-d?"

Keren, "I describe myself as a believer, and I do believe that my talent is a gift. I find the whole creative process is entwined with an energy, a feeling of dialogue, of a gift that I was given. Each collection, every idea, is a gift which I am thankful. I find myself in a relationship with some higher force, a form of energy which allows the creation to be expressed through me."

Tobi, "How does faith help society?"

Keren, "Being an artist, running a business, and creating are all complex processes. Feeling thankful, or grateful, believing that you are an emissary who is doing good by making women and brides beautiful on their wedding day, is a big part of what drives the creation and motivates me to continue doing what I love. The faith and the dream are an integrative part of the journey."

Tobi, "How do you define jewelry faith, brides and weddings?"

Keren, "I love the fact that I make brides happy, and I love being a part of the happiest day of their lives. It is a great privilege. Decorating women, creating beauty, is something that I delight in. For me, jewelry, is more than the piece itself. It is emotion, symbolism and strength combined."

Tobi, "I could discuss the 24 pieces of jewelry for a bride as mentioned in Sefer Geula (The book of Redemption Chapter 35), but I think I will save that for the next book.

If jewelry were a prayer, how would you design it?"

Keren, "I use my hands to create, and I find that there is a lot of strength when crafting by hand. I would use a hand motif, placing the hands in a prayer position, or a giving thanks position. I would also use the lip motif, a motif I use for lip jewelry, focusing on the power of our words when we talk, and while we pray."

There is enormous depth in Keren that goes beyond her exquisite crowns, rings, earrings, and necklaces, that beautifies her customers with much more than just the jewels themselves. They are a piece of herself that radiates from within to glorify the piece displayed on the outside.

The story of Chanah comes to mind when speaking with Keren. Chanah lived in the era before the temple was built in Jerusalem. She was the barren second wife of Elkanah. While his first wife Penina had seven children, Chanah remained a tragic and broken woman. Her intense prayers to G-d promised that if G-d gave her a child, she would gift it back to him. Her prayers were answered with her son Samuel, who became a prophet compared to Moses and Aaron in stature. Chanah prayed silently but her lips moved. From this gesture, the sages tell us that our obligation is to articulate our prayers and pronounce every word clearly. Praying silently during Shemoneh Esrai, the required 3 times a day prayer service, is a tribute to her. It was Chanah that unknowingly through her lips showed how men are obligated to pray, even today (women are not obligated). Her lip service added a greater understanding of our relationship to G-d. She refused to accept her limitations and asked for a personal blessing with the intention to fully serve G-d. Her fervent belief anticipated the direction her soon to be born son would take.

Keren Wolf Lip Collection and other works bejewels the out of the ordinary surfaces of the human form. She has created and touched unlikely areas, as the mouth with great beauty and excitement, leaving me with a sense of renewed meaning of the importance of a good lip.

Counting Sapphires

Napoleon did not have much money when he proposed to Josephine. He collected all the money he could for a beautiful sapphire and diamond ring on a gold band for his fiancé. In a design setting named "You and Me," the sapphire stones were only one carat each, yet they have a priceless historical value. With this ring she became Empress Josephine.

Until today, the most famous and beloved Royal engagement ring is the 18-carat diamond and sapphire stunner purchased in 1981 by Prince Charles for his then fiancé, Lady Diana. Prince William made it even more cherished when he proposed to Kate Middleton with his mother's ring, as a gesture of love and respect for his family's legacy.

The Logan Sapphire and The Star of Bombay are two of the world's most valuable sapphires. A flawless sapphire originating from Sri Lanka, the Logan Sapphire is one of the most famous gemstones in the world. It has a rich deep blue color and weighs 422.99 carats. It is the second biggest sapphire in the world. The enormous sapphire is named after Polly Logan, its original owner. In 1960, she donated it to the Smithsonian Institute. Currently, it is set in a brooch and surrounded by 20 round diamonds. It is on display at Washington D.C.'s Museum of Natural History.

The 182 carat Star of Bombay is violet blue. It was a gift to silent film star, Mary Pickford, by her husband, Douglas Fairbanks who was also a silent film star. She later bequeathed it to the Smithsonian Institute.

Elizabeth Taylor, one of Hollywood's greatest movie stars, was just as famous for her jewels. In 1952, her second husband to be, Michael Wilding, publicly proposed with a huge cabochon sapphire that started the trend of blue sapphire engagement rings.

I could continue with The Star of Asia in the Smithsonian, or St Edward's Sapphire that is part of the British Crown Jewels. It is believed that the stone was present in the coronation ring of Edward the Confessor whose reign in England started in 1042. Legend says that he was buried with it in Westminster Abbey.

What is so mesmerizing and intoxicating about this substance called sapphire? As always, I ask the bigger question. What does this have to do with Torah (Bible)? There is a clue in the time of the year that follows Passover and ends with Shavuot. Sapphires and Safira, the counting of the Omer have more in common than you think.

The period of the counting of the Omer is a time of potential for inner growth and character refinement (middot) through reflection and development of one aspect each day for the 49 days counted between Passover and Shauvot (a Jewish festival close in timing to Pentecost).

In Kabbalah, each of the seven weeks of the Omer-counting is associated with one of the seven lower sefirot (G-dly powers).

Chesed (loving-kindness)
Gevurah (might)
Tipheret (beauty)
Netzach (victory)
Hod (acknowledgment)
Yesod (foundation)
Malchut (kingdom)

Each day of each week is also associated with one of these seven sefirot, which creates forty-nine permutations.

The Hebrew word for sapphire is sapir. The Hebrew word sefirah has several meanings. The famous Kabbalist, the RaMak, in his monumental work the **Pardes** writes that sefirah comes both from the root mispar (number) and sipur, as in relating a story. A third root of sefirah is sapir, a sapphire stone, which is a translucent crystal that shines brightly.

The result of the Omer is the ultimate refined state we become to properly receive the Torah (Bible) from Hashem (G-d). The third holiday of the "Salosh regalim" is the grand finale of Shavuot (Jewish festival). All this work leads us to the glorious conclusion of Matan Torah, the arrival of "The Ten Commandments."

Both sets of tablets (luchos) were carved of sapphire stone. After Moshe (Moses) broke the first set, G-d revealed a large deposit of sapphire under his tent. He recycled some of the stone to carve the second tablets and was permitted to keep the remainder for his own personal riches (Rashi to Exodus 34:1).

Learning more about this divine stone in **Naviem** (Books of the Prophets) finds sapphire as the material used in Hashem's (G-d's) Throne of Glory. There are more kabbalistic thoughts about the stone having the power of wisdom and the third eye.

Before Napoleon Bonaparte went shopping for the perfect ring, or mining excavations in India yielded the most valuable sapphires in the world, the Torah (Bible) taught us the appreciation and value of this precious stone. The counting of the Omer is our chance to polish and perfect our own personal sapphire with daily thought and self-awareness. This allows us the 49 days of labor to prepare for Hashem (G-d) to grant us the privilege of receiving His Torah (Bible) written on the most glorious sapphire stones.

May Hashem (G-d) grant us all a collection of flawless, brilliantly blue, and perfectly polished paths to welcome Moshiach (Messiah) in our lifetimes.

A Monster in My Sukkah

The New York Times described Tzuri Gueta's jewelry as "blurring the lines between craft, fashion and art." In truth, that is a small statement with a large translation.

I met Tzuri during the first Bijoux Contemporary Show at The Norton Museum in Palm Beach, FL. He was a part of AIDA (Association of Israel's Decorative Arts) that hosted top Israeli jewelry artists to exhibit during the event. Aside from his immediate charm, his collection was whimsical, disturbing, and endearing. Tzuri Gueta had just completed his collaboration with Chanel on the label's Spring 2012 Collection. Every piece he brought was sold immediately. I cherish my blush-colored bracelet and earrings he designed that seemed to match everything perfectly.

Since 1989, Tzuri has continued to work with the most important fashion houses in Paris, Japan, and around the world such as Givenchy, Jean Paul Gaultier, Issey Miyake, Christian Lacroix and many other haute couture power houses.

Tzuri was born and educated in Israel. He graduated from the Shankar School of Design in Israel, which proudly ranks in the top ten fashion schools globally. He invented a fabric made of silicone and silk. This patented combination allows him to create magical jewelry, sculptures, accessories, and furniture.

I could not believe my eyes when I visited his Paris Salon with my daughter after her high school graduation. He gave us a tour of the workroom and the process of manufacturing the material he invented. Each piece was lovingly crafted by hand from inception to completion. We were both mesmerized by his world of color, creativity, and imagination.

Having grown up in a small beach town in Israel, his inspiration comes from the sea.

His designs reflect the memory and vision of the mysterious world that lies beneath the water. No words can describe the look, feel and vibrancy of each piece he creates. Every time I wear his jewelry people ask, "what is that?" with the wide-eyed enthusiasm of a child.

Tzuri answered my question about fusing faith into his unique medium. He explained,

"Faith has been incorporated in the process of my research in that when I start out on a project, I don't know in advance where it will lead me. I have faith that I will find a solution. I do not know where the research will lead me when I first start out, but I enter the process without knowing where I will go with it but with faith that the answer will come to me, that tomorrow what I want to happen will happen. I have only a general idea where I want to go, but as I go ahead things reveal themselves to me mystically, unexpectedly, and unconsciously. I think we must have a faith to create something personal."

I wondered, how would Tzuri Gueta interpret Day 5 of creation when G-d made the sea and all its wonderful creatures? In particular, the very largest of them all, the Tanninim.

Tanninim are Hashem's (G-d's) sea monsters, also known as Leviathan. They are introduced in Breishit, (Genesis) sentence 21 during G-d's weeklong creation of the world. Rashi mentions in the words of the Aggadah (Baba Bathra 74b), as it refers to the Leviathan (a particular kind of sea monster) and its mate, that G-d created both male and female. He slew the female and salted her away for the righteous in the future; for if they would multiply, they would destroy the world and disrupt its order.

Talmud (Baba Bathra 75a) it is written that the Leviathan sea creature will be slain. Its flesh or meat to be served as a feast to the righteous in the time of Moshiach (Messiah). It's skin or hide will be used to cover the tent where the sumptuous banquet will be held. The festival of Sukkot (Holiday of Booths) has a certain prayer that is recited upon leaving the sukkah. "May it be your will, Lord our G-d and G-d of our forefathers, that just as I have fulfilled and dwelt in this sukkah, so may I merit in the coming year to dwell in the sukkah of the skin of Leviathan next year in Jerusalem."

In Tehillim, chapter 74, King David writes "the sea with Your might; You shattered the heads of the sea monsters. You crushed the heads of Leviathan; You give it as food to the people in companies." The most thought provocative interpretation is the one of Rav. Abraham Isaac Kook, the first chief rabbi of Israel, Kabbalist, and a renowned Torah (Bible) scholar. He describes the Leviathan as a singular creature both male and female, "its tail is placed in its mouth" (Zohar) "twisting around and encompassing the entire world" (Rashi on Baba Batra 74b). This translation is a metaphor for the universe's underlying unity. This unity will only be revealed in the time of Moshiach when the righteous will feast on the Leviathan during the holiday of Sukkot.

Do Jewish women understand their immense power in Moshiach's welcoming event?

I must include another female who should sit on a throne in the Sukkah who could certainly be dressed in Tzuri 's unusual jewels such as a crown or scepter. The Talmud, Masechet Sukkah, explains that a famous wealthy Hasmonean Queen by the name of Helena, was known to have had grand sukkah frequently visited by important rabbis. In fact, it was her personal oversized sukkah of 20 cubits that was a highly discussed halachic (legal) debate. Was it too tall for the proper structure designed for the Feast of Tabernacles?

Rabbi Yehudah did not find it halachically (legally) problematic. However, different sages agree that women are not required to dwell in a sukkah since it is a time-bound commandment, and therefore the rabbis made no comment on the height of her sukkah because they thought the point was moot. Rabbi Yehudah argued that had Queen Helena's sukkah been problematic, the rabbis surely would have addressed the issue because she had seven sons who were required to dwell in it.

From her royal Sukkah story, we understand the greatness of Queen Helena, who exemplified the sacred task endowed to Jewish mothers throughout the ages, to embrace their children with the love of Torah (Bible). Queen Helena was not required to dwell in a sukkah, she nonetheless ensured that a proper sukkah was erected for her children, and she joined them in the mitzvah of the holiday.

Helena HaMalka (queen) is an ancient role model for women and mitzvot participation. She took on this voluntary mitzvah and this act was eternalized in Jewish law.

It seems that the exceptionally large sea monster has a big place in our future. Can women draw strength from an enormous sea creature? Can we draw strength from Queen Helena? It depends on how you see yourself. Are you a powerful force of nature, a reigning royal figure? Or are you a fictional Disney character, or a maiden in distress?

The Medieval Jews

It was my first visit to The Cloisters at The Metropolitan Museum of Art. I wanted to view the Jewish jewelry collection that was on loan there. I was greeted by the museum's jewelry head curator, Barbara Drake Boehm, who enthusiastically described the beauty and importance of the hidden treasures. "The Colmar Treasure, a medieval Jewish legacy" is tragically ironic to be here.

The Colmar Treasure consists of coins, jewels, and other accessories that were the precious possessions of a Jewish family who lived in medieval Alsace. They were hidden during the 14th century, buried inside the wall of a house in Colmar, France. It was once a thriving Jewish community that was scapegoated as the cause of the Plague and put to death when it struck the region with devastating ferocity in 1348.

On loan from The Musée de Cluny, Paris, the Colmar Treasure is displayed alongside select works from The Met Cloisters and little-known

Judaica from collections in the United States and France. Although the objects are without the usual "bling" they are small in scale and few. The collection attempts to overturn popular views of medieval Europe as entirely a monolithic Christian place. The exhibition points to both legacy, and loss, by acknowledging the prominence of the Jewish minority community, in the tumultuous 14th century, who were falsely accusing of being responsible for the Bubonic Plague in Europe.

As their punishment, The Bishop, and The Lords, ordered Jews to be burned to death, and those who tried to escape were caught by peasants and murdered, all in the name of the Catholic Church.

A few pieces of jewelry, that testify to Jewish life there, miraculously survived by being hidden in the walls of a house during the 14th century. They remained there for over 500 years. For years, little was written about this incredible find. However, decades later, after much of the treasure was purchased by the Musée de Cluny, historians found an obvious clue. One of the rings, a marvel of gold and colored enamel, featured the Hebrew letters for "Mazel tov." This matrimonial ring, shaped like the Bais Hamikdash (temple), confirmed that the ring was Jewish.

"The ring is so beautiful, so refined," the exhibition and Met Cloister's senior curator Barbara Drake Boehm told the "Times of Israel." The delicacy of the goldsmithing is extraordinary. The roof over the base of the ring is done like an open, delicate architectural arcade, with capitals and columns holding up the domed roof."

Another piece, a sapphire, ruby and pearl brooch, was a Tznuit (modesty) pin to be used as a deterrent to unwanted gestures by men. It served as a bejeweled warning to men not to touch women improperly. A Shabbos Key made of silver was also a piece of jewelry that can be used on Shabbos without violating the Halacha (law) of carrying.

A Toadstone ring made of fossilized fish tooth was used to ward off the Aiyen Harah (evil eye). There are also various components of garment hooks and eyes, belt buckles and buttons which were all testaments of wealth and taste.

The exhibit leaves you with a taste of an important Jewish presence during the medieval times in Europe. It also leaves you with an enormously heavy heart for the demise and elimination of Jews during that time.

As I headed to the gift shop to purchase a catalog, I could not help but be annoyed by the Catholic imagery that occupies most of the space at The Cloisters. It seemed so strange to see this exhibit in these surroundings. Perhaps it is an attempt to garner forgiveness, perhaps it is a reminder that during these times of reemerging antisemitism that it has all happened done before. This time, we are experiencing hate fueled by ignorance. Tweets and posts by political officials, activists, and extreme stupidities are the new normal.

My hope is that we learn something unbelievably valuable from this small collection of Jewish jewelry. We remember that hate toward the Jewish people has not changed throughout the years, it just gets updated. The justification for our elimination seems to reinvent itself generation after generation.

My hope is that we, as Jews, will outlive our past persecutions and that the hatred that caused them will not. We look forward to a bejeweled future where we never need to hide our treasures again.

Shattered Vessels

If the Crown Jewels could be reinterpreted into shapes of glass, Nirit Dekel's jewelry could be used in a royal coronation. Nirit is one of Israel's jewelry artisan superstars. We were first introduced in 2009 at Loot, The Museum of Art and Design's jewelry fair.

I had just been through an exceedingly difficult time and Nirit gifted me a crystal ice necklace that thoroughly lifted my spirits. Aside from the great kindness she displayed, I bow to her wisdom in color, craft, and shape.

In the year 2000, Nirit visited Dale Chihuly's exhibition at David's Tower in Jerusalem. Leaving Israel's high-tech world, she was struck by the enormous glass works. "It was like an alarm clock waking me back to life. I was drawn as a magnet to the glass and immediately fell in love with it." She is fascinated by glass in its ability to be shaped and rearranged from everyday practicality to delicate pieces of artistic expression.

Nirit Dekel expresses a refreshing outlook in her glass beaded jewelry with whimsical, mysterious, outrageous, delicate, and colorful works. Using the traditional method of lamp working in Italian Moretti glass, she spins her genius into one-of-a-kind pieces.

She explains, "I define myself as both an artist and an artisan, as my point of view shifts and transforms. I work with my hands, manipulating the material by crafting trial and error. On one hand, I create objects that have functions, wearable pieces. On the other, I view every piece as a message carrier, a way to transmit my thoughts and ideas to the world."

I am drawn to the Torah (Bible) connection to these magnificent glass jewelry pieces. The realization of what that is came from another of her quotes from a recent interview about her exhibition with FROOTS Gallery. She answered a question about her artistic process that contained interesting biblical hints, "For me, the material is the origin of creation. I find myself drawn to the glass, and the entire creative process evolves from there, until the creation of a complete piece of jewelry. I find that every glass bead is important in relation to the finished piece, it does not carry any significance on its own, but receives new meaning as part of whole."

In Kabbalah, we explore the act of "the shattering of the vessels" (imagined as glass) containing Hashem's (G-d's) infinite light. This teaches us to how redesign our thoughts to address what lies ahead of us.

Before the creation of the lower worlds could proceed, as depicted in Berishis (Genesis), the prospect that the lower worlds would receive Divine Light opposed the other goal of Creation. That other goal was man retaining man's freewill. As the ARI explains (Etz Chaim 8:6), if G-d's infinite light is always with us, man would not have free will. G-d therefore conceals His Light, and in doing so allowed man to choose freely between good and evil. Therefore, the original glass vessels had to be shattered for the light was too much to bear.

From the shattering, shards were thrown into Creation and formed Kelipot (forces of evil). The existence of these Kelipot creates a balance of good and evil in Creation, enabling man to have free choice. Allowing the Ten Sefirot of Hashem's (G-d's) presence to act side by side with the Kelipot.

This a deep thought process to connect to a mere necklace or bracelet, but Nirit's work has enormous depth even if it appears at times as bright and comical.

Her pieces take on a divine glow as the image of Hashem's (G-d's) vessels of light. Yet, some designs appear as the images of Kelipot shards hanging delicately from your neck. The greatest compliment to a true artist is that their work evokes deep thought. Nirit's jewelry contains many Kabbalistic thoughts put together into one great piece of jewelry.

The Earrings of the Emirates

Part of the teachings of Rebbe Nachman of Breslov is that one should plan on a great outcome when in a state of great pain. In fact, during great sorrow, one should already plan their victory. Throughout my chemotherapy sessions, PET scans, blood tests and eventual surgery, I kept focusing on a huge event that I planned since my diagnosis. The party to honor the next chapter of my life themed, "Remission in Dubai." All my girlfriends and prayer warriors started planning their wardrobes at the end of 2020, envisioning our big trip in mid-2021.

When I first visited Dubai in November 2008, for a jewelry show, I was warned about midday sandstorms and Lamborghini taxis. I was not prepared for the exaggerated opulence. Simply put, Dubai is Las Vegas on alien steroids. When anyone asks me to explain the region, I simply reply, "I still cannot wrap my head around air conditioning units that rise from the sand to cool you on your beach lounge chairs."

Skiing in a life size snow globe in the middle of the largest luxury mall in the world, paled only to The Jewelry Show at the Dubai Convention Center. The sea of black burkas and priceless crocodile Hermès Kelly bags was strong sign that uber luxury was the most important calling card for this crowd of attendees.

As I strolled around the booths surveying the baubles being salivated over, I saw a big crowd gathering at one vendor, Tutti-Frutti from Italy. They displayed a candy store of fanciful multicolored earrings in all shapes and sizes from small to outrageous. Since I love big earrings, I grabbed a pair of carved white mother-of-pearl with ruby and diamonds that were about 3 inches long. At my side was a woman dressed in the black uniform, handbag, and diamond Rolex. She grabbed the same earrings while her mother-in-law stood close guard.

I immediately asked her, "I don't mean to sound disrespectful, but where in the world do you wear these earrings if you are always covered from head to toe?" My friend laughed at this encounter as the young woman grabbed her cell phone (iPhone 100) and showed me pictures of herself without the Burka. I was shocked and we began a great conversation. Turns out there are "girl parties" at the separate country clubs where women show off their jewelry and everything else. She invited "us girls" to attend and see for ourselves. Her mother-in-law was getting agitated at our delightful girl chatter. The "shvigah" (mother-in-law) was sporting a solid gold face piece that demanded nothing but respect and reverence. I have shared this story so many times as an example of the common ground between women no matter what their background. Girls will be girls.

Dubai and I have a lot in common. We love our jewelry. In 2007, a series of postage stamps were issued there with designs of traditional women's jewelry, in association with the Sharjah Museums. There is even a designated market, Dubai Gold Souk or Gold Soukis, that is a traditional bazaar. It houses over 380 retailers, most of which are traders of gold, platinum, and diamond jewelry.

The Arab culture has shown me some interesting places that jewelry can be worn. There is an item of jewelry, mainly of gold, for a every part of the body in this culture. These items showcase the styles and history of women's jewelry within that region.

Gard al hel: Bracelet made in gold or silver that may be used by married women or grown-up girls for the wrist.

Al Zunaid: Bracelets used for the upper arm.

Al Khanasir: Rings worn around the little finger.

Al Shawahid: Rings worn on index finger.

Al Khalkhal: Gold or silver bracelets worn above the ankle.

Al Fatakh: Rings worn on big toe on either or both feet.

Mariya Um Al Nairat: A gold necklace.

Mortasha: A thick ornamental gold necklace.

Shaghab Bu Shouk: Embellished gold earrings.

Bushuq: A gold bracelet.

Tassah: Jewels for the forehead.

Jewelry

    I cannot wait to stay at any one of the luxurious hotels like The Burj and dine on kosher food at Armani Privé at the Armani Hotel. My girl's party trip will take full advantage of all the great tourist sites and activities. We may treat ourselves to some authentic Emirates jewelry, then hop on a direct flight to Tel Aviv.

Photo courtesy Liat Ginzberg

Jewelry

Photo courtesy Liat Ginzberg

Photo courtesy of Keren Wolf

Jewelry

Photo courtesy of Keren Wolf

The House of Faith and Fashion

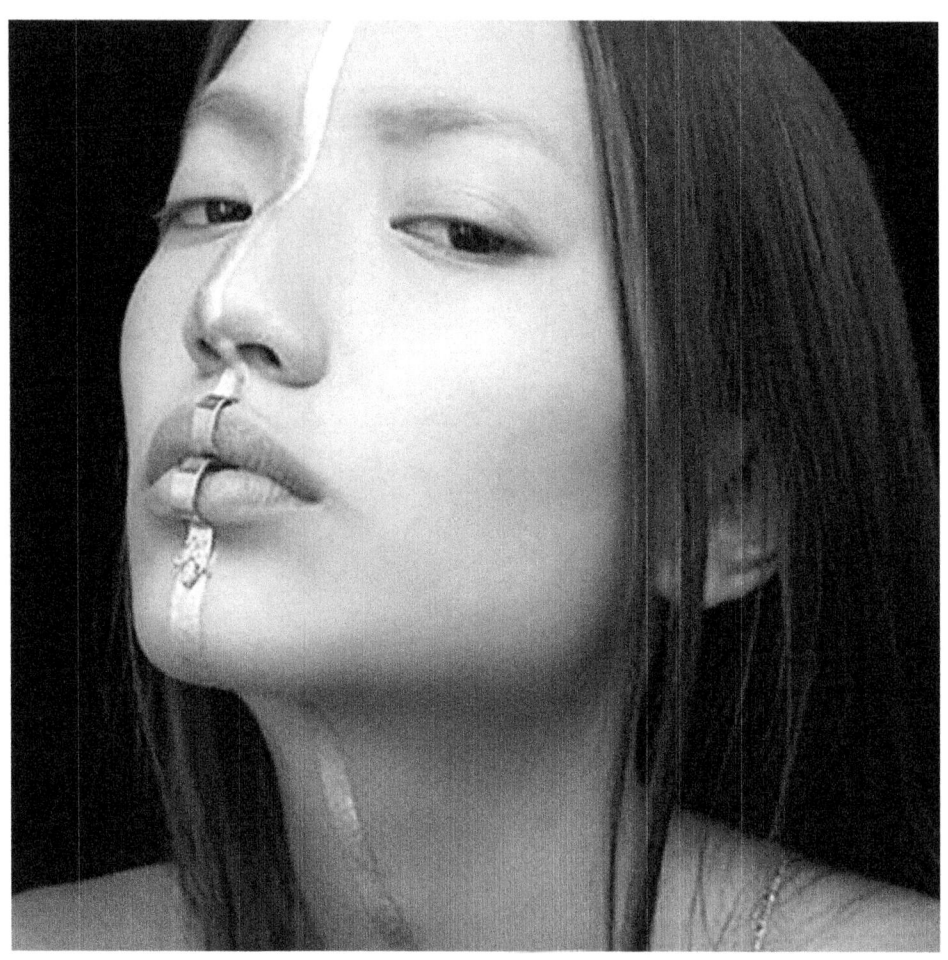

Photo courtesy of Keren Wolf

Jewelry

Photo courtesy of Tzuri Gueta

Photo courtesy of Tzuri Gueta

Jewelry

Photo courtesy Nirit Dekel

Photo courtesy Nirit Dekel

Jewelry

Photo courtesy Nirit Dekel

The House of Faith and Fashion

The Earrings of the Emirates

Jewelry

Bracelets by Cathie Underwood, Gifts of Grace Designs

CHAPTER 3
STYLE & BEAUTY

"The true power, beauty and value of a person is not indicated by where they are standing, but in the direction they are facing."
Rav Doniel Katz founder of The Elevation Project

Style & Beauty

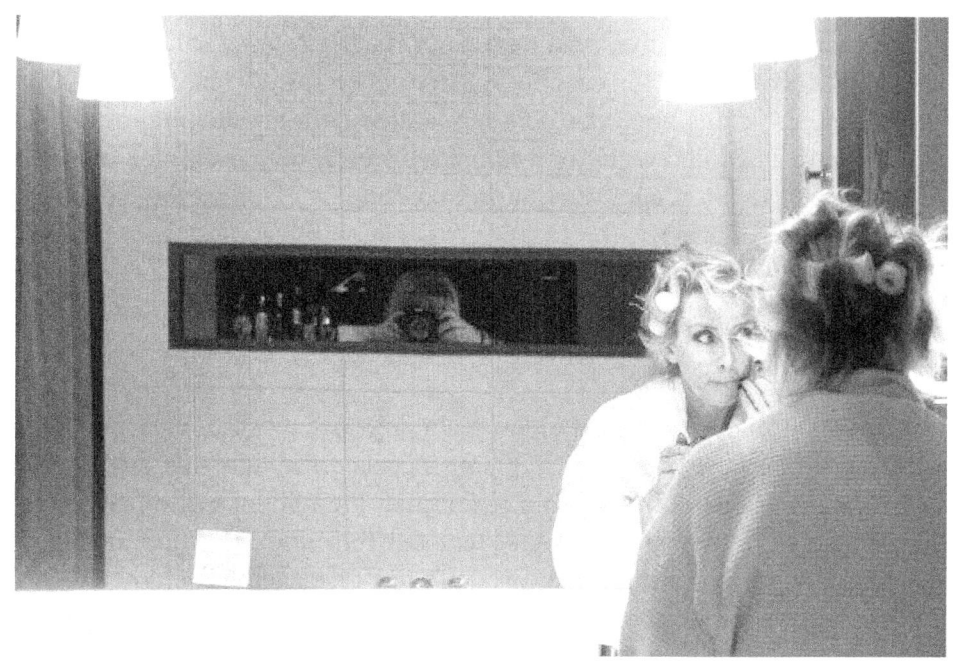

Tobi Rubinstein by Lola Rubinstein

Have a Beautiful Day

As I lay in bed at 2:11 am, I am awake with a body pumped full of steroids to stop the dreadful pain experienced after chemotherapy. This is round two in the journey towards remission of stage IV cancer. Strangely, today was my most self-recognizable day in months. Today I had the same energy that I had pre sickness. Since it is Thursday, my Shabbos prep had me preparing all the festive foods then setting my table with my favorite dishes, stemware, cloths, napkins, and flowers. I spent an hour on the stationary bicycle while returning my calls required post treatment. I ate a healthy salad and drank my Ginger Kombucha to resupply nutrient energies. Then, I finished an entire chapter of this book and felt exhilarated with my accomplishments. The evening was filled with my usual playlist of Torah (Bible) lectures and text messages to my prayer warrior group of angels. This was not a normal post-chemo day for me.

How could today be such a beautiful day? How can sickness turn into beauty?

I have surrendered to G-d since receiving this disease, as I fight this cancer. It has been a strange blessing because through this situation, I have found my true purpose. I no longer fear the opinions of others or the acceptance of my behavior. I only fear not fulfilling the true purpose of my life. The peace of mind that my faith has given me has eradicated the upheaval that I initially felt when my doctor said, "you have cancer."

The shock has amplified my faith in G-d and his plan for me. Cancer brought me to an elegant state of introspection. I am studying where my life trauma began and grew over the years. The repeated mistakes, the triggers, the manipulators, the heart breakers, all having too many important roles in my life. They occupied and developed unhealthy spaces in my body. I think my life has been a divinely orchestrated and curated mistake ridden plan. Rarely did I turn to G-d for help or comfort in prayer, always babbling the words and never understanding their worth or meaning. Over the last ten years, I have had a complete reversal of heart and soul, which probably prepared me for this unexpected chapter. I am now fighting for my life, with a clearer understanding of the rollercoaster ride I finally jumped off. I am filled with gratitude that G-d brought me to the life I have now before my fight with cancer began.

How can you find beauty in disease? By finding beauty in your true purpose. By finding beauty that surrounds you during your fight. By finding beauty in gratitude to G-d for the things He gave to help you fight. By finding beauty in the company of friends, family, clergy, and doctors that surround you with love, support and proper care for your body, mind, and soul. The real beauty is to be found in surrender to G-d, for it is only He that heals us.

My favorite book, "The Ethics of the Fathers," (2:1) explains it best. Rabbi said, "Which is the proper path for man to choose for himself? Whatever brings beauty to the person that does it and is beautiful to mankind." Rabbi Yehudah Hanassi emphasizes the balance of doing what is beautiful and beneficial for his/her own spiritual growth. At the same time focusing that spiritual growth on others.

Beauty in Hebrew is tiferet which means a harmony of opposites. Beauty is found in the center of two opposing thought processes, good and bad. Beauty can be defined as vain or as spiritual. True beauty is found in the existence of both. That I can have a serious disease and still feel beautiful is a composite of opposites, but it is the beautiful truth.

No Face or New Face

I can no longer ignore the fading faces of Jewish women in "religious media" outlets. Advertisements for medical clinics have the image of a female doctor replaced by a cabbage patch doll. A real estate brochure for a new family development in Jerusalem has only pictures of daddy and no mommy.

There are too many flyers for charity events honoring a particular Mr. and Mrs. with only a male picture. However, the most ridiculous example is the half-time Super Bowl LIV performance with a male singer bamboozling the audience about the joys and pains of motherhood, a song that is sung by women, about women. Somewhere in the video, there was a faded female form. Thankfully, there are sensitive and informative organizations that highlight this harmful practice. Chochamat Nashim is leading the way to re-educate and rescue the women from the current trend of the missing female face.

On the other end of the spectrum, there remains the endless need for women to be beautiful. That does not require erasing the image but enhancing and preserving it. Outside of an Instagram filter, photoshop, or pure magic, plastic surgery is the method of ageless beauty. Botox, lasers, fillers, nips, and tucks are all part of the path to forever young and beautiful. I am not denying that one can grow old gracefully and I accept what G-d has designed as the aging process. The pursuit of perfection in beauty has been an issue for Jewish women for as long as I can remember. Let us start with the infamous nose. In my day, it was a rite of passage to get rhinoplasty with a prominent surgeon including his signature turned up design.

A few years ago, on a Shabbos (sabbath), a very prominent Rebbetzin (Rabbi's wife) whispered into my ear at the kiddush (food) table, "What did you do to your face and who is your doctor?"

So, let us talk plastic surgery and Torah/Halacha (law). With an increasing number of Jewish women opting for plastic surgery, the demand is greater than ever. The new "Woman of Valor" wants a "maintenance" plan to keep her young and beautiful. Yes, she will continue to sew, cook, sell in the marketplace, and bring joy to her family, but she needs her eyes done, face lifted, and neck smoothed.

Judaism is a huge proponent of inner beauty. Just read the words of "Aishes Chayil" (woman of valor) and you will get the gist of it. However, the psychological meaning to beauty is not to be ignored. Reading an article in "YNET News" gave a quick overview of the Halacha (legal) aspect. Rabbi Eliezer Yehuda Waldenberg and Rabbi Moshe Feinstein viewed these surgeries as a danger to the patient, and since the Torah (Bible) forbids man from putting himself at risk for no reason, they prohibited needless surgeries. However, there are some rabbis, including Rabbi Ovadia Yosef, who considered the fact that medicine is advancing all the time. He also understood that an aesthetic flaw is no less important than any other physical flaw, like a scar from an accident. Today, it is understood that how a person feels about herself is significant, because it affects her deeply. Rav Ovadia's made a sensitive ruling on this subject. He set the grounds on how to search for the right plastic surgeon.

I have known Dr. David Shafer for over 13 years and had the privilege to ask him some deep questions about his career path as a leading plastic surgeon. He has been interviewed on countless television shows, in print articles and reality shows worldwide, but I do not think he was ever approached with these questions.

Tobi, "Do you think your talent is G-d given, or do you often feel like a G-d?"

Dr. Shafer, "We all have G-d given talents. That is what makes us individuals. Certainly, I have worked hard to achieve success and I have been fortunate to be surrounded by supportive and loving family and friends. However, there is an element of something higher or a guiding light. How was I able to jump through every hoop, clear every obstacle, and always land on my feet?

I stand where I am today as a kid from a small town in Michigan and now have a three-floor plastic surgery penthouse in NYC. I think people when they forget what they have been given and start to think they are G-d. A professor once told me that when everything is going right, when you feel omnipotent, when you are on the top of the world, you get a tap on your shoulder from G-d to remind you to stay grounded."

Tobi, "Has plastic surgery replaced the appropriate sense of self?"

Dr Shafer, "The question is what defines self? Is it our physical, or mental being, or the culmination of all our traits, both tangible and abstract? We do not live in a vacuum and we change over time. G-d has given us the ability to adapt, change course, and redefine our destiny. Plastic surgery is just another tool we use to express ourselves. As a plastic surgeon, I have a responsibility to use my skills responsibly. One thing I tell my patients is that sometimes it's my job to say no."

Tobi, "Is plastic surgery the new faith?"

Dr. Shafer, "Certainly, people find faith in many ways. Plastic Surgery gives people power, unlocks their inner self. My goal is to find a balance for people. To make sure they are not chasing false or unrealistic expectations, while also providing safe and effective guidance and treatments. To give power to each person to define themself."

Tobi, "How do you feel about altering G-d's creation, or are you are just enhancing it?"

Dr. Shafer, "The guiding principle of medicine is first do no harm. All plastic surgery is to help the patient whether reconstructive surgery after breast cancer, or a mommy makeover after childbirth. Our bodies are dynamic and change over time in response to genetics and the environment. My approach to beauty and aesthetics is not just skin deep. My new clinic focuses on three levels. They are plastic surgery for physical and structural treatments, our Skin & Laser Lab for skin rejuvenation and my Metabolic Aesthetics Center for beauty treatments at the cellular level with IV therapy, hormone balancing and peptide enhancement. A person's sense of self and G-d's image remains constant. It's their expression of self that makes us unique and I am there to help them."

Dr. David Shafer is an A-list surgeon educated at Mayo Clinic. He is speaking on a true level of Torah (Bible). His professionalism and respect for G-d's holy masterpiece is something that provides his patients with belief and comfort in his work.

However, here I am confronting opposites. No images versus a constantly improving image and no face versus an updated face. Erasing G-d's work versus enhancing G-d's work. Which one is healthier? I certainly opt for the improved version (if it needs improving), rather than eliminating a version.

"A handsome person is in a better position to influence others. One who seeks to influence others for the better should therefore take care that his appearance is attractive." (Mieri; The Rebbe in Biurim). Shine beautiful, bright, and bold and see what great influence you can have on the outside world.

Crystal Water Glasses

Crystal glass stemware deserves a place at any holiday table, and it pays tribute to the single most influential woman in the Torah (Bible).

I adore Baccarat, although I still have not collected a full service of 12. I make do with the brands like Mikasa, Lenox, and Waterford. That does not keep me from dreaming about the twelve perfect deep red, multi-cut, tall wine goblets that dress the table of my fantasies.

Baccarat was established in 1765 by the Bishop of Metz who wished to encourage industry in the little village of Baccarat, 250 miles east of Paris, France. It has grown tremendously to captivate the luxury brand market in countless other categories, including hotels.

If you got the impression that I am wild about my shoes, I am equally wild about my table scape. For now, I will focus on the water goblet.

Two years ago, Rabbanit Dr. Adena Berkowitz wrote her own Haggadah (Passover recitation) called "The Jewish Journey Haggadah." In it she proclaimed there should be a glass of water placed on the seder plate to honor Miriam and her holy and aquatic achievements.

This goblet would be designated Kos Miryam. I asked Rabbanit Adena her reason for this non-traditional custom. She shared that it is, "a reminder of Moshe's powerful sister. She rescued him from the water, and G-d gave her the well of water that sustained the Jewish people throughout their journey in the desert. Later, the well of waters dried up, cementing Miriam as the only worthy person to have such G-dly validation."

She shared her source for recognizing Miriam's role at the seder can be found in the suggestion made in during the 10th century by Rav Sherira, the Gaon of Pumpedita in Babylonia. The people of Kair Ovan in North Africa asked him about the significance of the two foods Jews place at the seder. These are an egg and a shank bone. He told them they symbolize the two messengers, Moshe (Moses) and Aharon, (Aaron) who G d sent to Egypt. But he continued there are those who also place a fish on the seder table in memory of Miriam. He referenced the verse from Micah 6:4, "And I will send before you Moshe and Aharon and Miriam." We learn from tradition that these three food items, the egg, meat, and fish will be eaten in the world to come.

I needed that feminine twist to Passover, beyond the cooking, cleaning, and shopping, as a breath of fresh air. My Passover seder included a light blue cut- crystal filled with water positioned next to Eliyahu's traditional one.

If you think of Miriam today, you could see her as the ultimate "Girl Boss" influencer, who might have millions of followers on her Instagram, Twitter, and Facebook pages.

I am fortunate to partake in Yitzy Weinberg's Thursday evening lectures on Zoom. They are part of my end of week routine. I am an enthusiastic student as I send him my notes afterwards. He sent me his dvar Torah

(Torah essay) on The Life and Legacy of Miriam. After reading it the fifth time, I asked if I could include it in this essay. Here it is.

"This should come as no surprise, since Targum (Micha 6, 4) writes that Miriam was the teacher of the Jewish women. The gemara says (Sotah 11b) that the Jewish people were taken out of Mitzrayim (slavery in Egypt) in merit of the righteous women of the generation. This reflects how Miriam's leadership was effective even at a time that Jewish males were struggling bitterly with their faith.

The steadfast faith of the Jewish women at that time is also reflected in that the passuk (Shemos 15, 20) describes the instruments used by Miriam and the women in saying Shira after kriyas yam suf. Rashi (ibid) explains that the women were so certain that miracles would be performed that they chose to bring musical instruments with them as they left Egypt to sing and dance whenever those miracles would manifest."

Her holy influence effected the women's behavior as reflected in (Shemos 32, 2). Jewish women refused to hand over their jewelry for the construction of The Golden Calf."

The Pirkei D' Rebbi Eliezer (Ch. 45) explains how the women did not get caught up in the moment and refused their husbands' demands, to the point that their husbands had to grab it by force. For their defiance, the women were rewarded with celebrating Rosh Chodesh, which represents constant renewal, the most vital mindset which enables someone to refrain from getting lost in life's moments."

"Miriam's great influence extended to the entire nation and its limited rebellious characters. Only one Jewish male found the passion and integrity to openly protest the making of the golden calf, for which he was murdered. This individual was Chur, the son of Miriam (Rashi to Shemos 32, 6 based on Tanchuma 20)."

You could say that Miriam exuded strength of character and even possessed some superpowers that today's Wonder Woman would envy. She formed a protective shield around the nation of Israel all the way back to when she demanded her parents remarry after their divorce. Proclaiming with certainty that her future brother Moses would set the divinely planned process of freedom in motion.

Hashem (G-d) knew exactly who to choose to when he picked Miriam, as she grew from Aaron's sister to Miriam the Leader, full of endless faith and determination.

As far as I am concerned, she is worthy of all the Baccarat crystal goblets one can fit on their seder table.

The Reflection of a Mirror

"Mirror, mirror on the wall, who is the fairest of them all?" chanted the evil queen in Snow White. In another famous novel, we see how enchanted and disappointed Alice was when she entered The Looking Glass. Mirrors have an interesting place in our psyche. Do they hold truth, vanity, mystery, or divinity?

The most lavish example of reflective madness is The Hall of Mirrors in the Versailles Castle in France. The principal feature of this hall is the seventeen mirror-clad arches that reflect the seventeen arcaded windows that overlook the exquisite gardens. Each area is composed of twenty-one mirrors with a total of 357 used in the decoration of the "Galerie des Glaces."

This ostentatious room is a statement of glory and ego constructed by a King that needed to compete with G-d himself. It is a hall of self-importance and nobility only a Ruler of men can make himself believe in. King Louis' mirrors s memorialize his great accomplishments as the King of France. Many other attributes of the Hall of Mirrors were lost to war for financial purposes, such as the silver table pieces and gueridons, which were melted by the order of Louis XIV in 1689 to finance a war.

Are mirrors holy? Can a mirror reflect divinity? Mirrors are reflections of self yet can be used for Hashem's (G-d's) glory. This possibility comes from the Torah (Bible).

Exodus 38:8 tells us that the bronze laver (washing basin) and its base of bronze of the Mishkin were made from the mirrors of, "the women who served at the entrance to the tent of meeting." The Jewish women used highly polished brass and other metals during their time as slaves in Egypt. Their mirrors were the only materials allowed to be utilized in Hashem's (G-d's) washing station for the Priests (Kohanim). The most important servants to G-d were required to rinse and prepare themselves in this area of the Mishkin and continue building King Solomon's Holy Temple (bais Hamikdash).

According to the Ibn Ezra, the basin, is given limitless dimensions because every single mirror donated had to be used in its construction no matter how big it would become. This shows the importance of these mirrors to Hashem (G-d). What was so special about them that not even one could be excluded from the construction?

A brilliant answer in the Midrash Tanchuma states that the donators were the mothers of many children, and the mirrors represented their faith and commitment to the continuation of Judaism for generations to come. Who were these brave mothers and how did they accomplish this?

When Bnei Yisrael (Jewish people) were enslaved in Egypt, Pharaoh deliberately kept the men away from their wives so that no children would be born, and the Jewish Nation would cease to exist. The Jewish men were in an exhausted state of depression and could not bring themselves to father children who would ultimately enter a world of slavery. However, the women did not fall to that thinking. They used their mirrors to attract and seduce their husbands so that the Jewish People would continue to multiply.

On another level, the women used their precious mirrors to alter their men's vision. A mirror primarily reflects however, it also narrows the field of vision. Looking into the mirrors, the men could see the Jewish reality, not the helpless backdrop of enslavement. It was that vision they needed to focus on, to see past their present reality into a better future.

When the women rushed to bring their mirrors to build the Mishkin, all the mirrors were required to be used; therefore, the Jewish women's reflective faith was represented in the building of Hashem's (G-d's) home.

Mirror, mirror on the wall, who is the fairest of them all? Every woman is Hashem's (G-d's) eyes is the answer.

Pageant Girls

When I first met Aviad Arik Herman, we were challenged to present a big and bold fashion statement about the Negev desert in Israel during New York Fashion Week 2017. I knew of his talents from the enormous press that his "Jerusalem of Gold Dress," worn by Miri Regev, received at The Cannes Film Festival. It was a daring and important message cementing Jerusalem as the capital of Israel. It was a defiant act using style which appeared on the global film stage and consumed the media. How many people can achieve that?

Aviad is charming, in a boyish way, with a fierce sense of style and purpose. Born in Ber Sheva, Israel, he is a self-taught designer who grew up carefully watching his mother and grandmother create dresses for themselves. He translated his thoughts and feelings into fanciful dresses. He has achieved international acclaim as a performing artist and fashion designer, equipped by his experience in costume design for dance, theatre, and beauty pageants.

In 2013, he was named the head designer for Miss Universe Sweden. He also designed costumes for Miss World Denmark, Miss World Israel, Miss Universe Israel & Miss Universe Austria, demonstrating his ability to dress international women. His outstanding designs gained further notoriety when Miss Germany 2014 was nominated for the Top 5 Best Costumes at the 63rd Miss Universe Pageant. Best National Costume was awarded to Miss Sweden at Miss Earth 2016. He is probably designing another award-winning costume right now.

His interest in the beauty of Israel has been translated into many collaborations with the pageants that Israel participates in. In 2016, and 2017, Miss World and Miss Universe Israeli representatives were designed for by Aviad with inspiration and tribute to Shoshana Damarion, the queen of Hebrew music and a Yemeni style icon. He used fifteen thousand Swarovski crystals to adorn the biblical Eve costume for Miss Universe. 2017 was the year of the new **Wonder Woman** film and Gal Gadot (Miss Universe Israel 2004) rose to superstardom as this superhero. That supernatural piece was nominated for the Top 5 Best Costumes for Miss Universe.

His work continues in Thailand, home of Miss Universe 2018. He is already starting to prepare for future pageants. Eurovision Song Contest winner NETTA, loved the beautiful kimono that he made for her Stockholm show. Israeli Pop Star Maya Buskila, who competed in the ESC 2019, graced the cover of "Israel Today" newspaper dressed in one of his designs. I cannot keep up with his pageants and theatre productions because there are more than I can write about.

What does a beauty pageant have to do with the Torah (Bible)? Could there be a connection between a beauty coronation and Hashem (G-d)?

Every year the spectacle of Miss Universe is watched by millions who do not know the first and greatest pageant was held in Shushan, the ancient capital of the Elamite empire (present day Iran). The winner of that contest would reign not for just twelve months, but for the rest of her life over an empire that reached "from India even unto Ethiopia, over a hundred and twenty-seven provinces." (Megillah Esther 1:1). The girl who won that beauty competition could not have known her name was to become famous throughout the world. She was destined to become the instrument of G-d who directed her movements and ultimately saved the entire Jewish nation.

At the heart of the Purim story is a lavish, decadent, and glamorous search for the most beautiful girl in Achasveros's Kingdom. Esther, as its winner, was crowned the Ruler's Queen, advisor, wife, and mother of his children.

Esther had a son, Darius, who became King Darius II. She raised him to be favorable to the Jews and he eventually lifted the ban against the rebuilding of the Beit Hamikdash (Holy Temple), which ushered the building of the Second Temple. What a glorious outcome to this pageant, far better than a glittering sash and a wave.

Aviad shared his admiration for modest practices of orthodox women. Suggesting that their innovation with fashion is challenging but rewarding.

Tobi, "Do you think your talent is G-d given?"

Aviad, "I do believe that talent is G-d given."

Tobi, "How does faith incorporate into your work?"

Aviad, "In my work, just as in the way I live my life, faith is mostly incorporated by showing up to the opportunities that come my way. I do believe they come for a reason and I always aim to do my best at any task along with my faith and trust in the team of people that help me achieve it."

Tobi, "Do you find spirituality in beauty pageants?"

Aviad, "I find something quite powerful and spiritual in the fact that underneath all the makeup, hairspray, and spectacular gowns are amazing young ladies who are passionately committed to becoming a better version of themselves to inspire and empower others as well."

The Torah (Bible) teaches us that inner and outer modesty is a women's true royal cloth by enabling, embracing, and nurturing every woman to be a Miss Universe in her own realm.

Aviad has a G-d given talent to make beauty queens but only G-d has the power to make authentic beauties out of beauty queens.

It is a Dog's Life

An Israeli study authored by Dr. Michel Balaish, Director of the Veterinary Institute at the Ministry of Agriculture & Rural Development, has discovered that the blood pressure of children who had a dog at home was lower than children who live without one, according to Israeli media.

The number of dogs adopted, fostered, or bought during the worldwide COVID-19 pandemic lockdowns were staggering. Owning and caring for a dog dramatically reduces our social isolation and fulfills our emotional needs.

Interaction with our dogs changes the hormone levels in our bodies as well as boost our mood.

Just three to five minutes of cuddling increases the wellbeing hormone endorphin, releases the happy hormone dopamine, and the love hormone oxytocin, while also reducing the stress hormone cortisol. Pets are the best natural painkillers.

Dog owners also benefit from reduced triglyceride levels, lower blood pressure, and have a lower risk of cardiovascular disease. I have my own testimony of my dog's devotion, undivided attention. and unconditional love during my journey fighting cancer. My dog knows instinctively when I am in pain and exactly where the pain originates. She has become my head nurse, making sure everyone is aware of my health status for the day. Her devotion is endless as she cries at my every trip to chemotherapy and licks my face when she picks me up afterwards.

Jewish tradition does not expressly prohibit keeping of dogs as pets, but biblical and rabbinic sources do include numerous references that associate dogs with violence and uncleanliness and do not suggest one be a part of the household.

Dogs are, for the most part, portrayed negatively in the Torah (Bible). Deuteronomy appears to equate dogs and prostitution, ruling in Deuteronomy 23:19 that if one of these is used to pay for an animal say, if one offered a dog or sex in exchange for a goat, that purchased animal cannot be brought to the temple as a sacrifice. The Book of Kings includes several references to dogs feeding on corpses. And in the Psalms, dogs are described as beasts that maul at human beings.

The Shulchan Aruch (a 16th-century legal code) takes a somewhat less restrictive approach, saying only that an "evil dog" must be bound in iron chains. Similarly, Rabbi Moshe Isserles, a 16th-century Polish scholar also known as the Rema, in his commentary on the Shulchan Aruch, writes that a dog that is liable to harm people must be kept chained.

This all sounds quite gruesome if you own a poodle.

Thank G-d, the notable 16th century Jewish leader, the Maharsha, says that a dog is a creature of love. He certainly saves the day by interpreting the dogs Hebrew name "kelev" which is etymologically derived from the words "kulo lev," or "all heart" (Rabbi Shmuel Eidels, Chidushei Aggadot, Sanhedrin 97a).

In the story of Adam and Eve's children, Cain and Able, Hashem (G-d) gave Cain a dog when he became a wanderer. This is in the Medrash, in Breishis (Genesis) Raba 22:12. The Ramban elaborates on this dog and human relationship. Cain was given a dog because he was afraid the animals would kill him, so he was given one of them to show the way, and wherever it went he knew it was ordained by Hashem (G-d) and he would not be killed there.

Hashem's (G-d's) blessing of the dog in Shemot 11:7, "And for all the Jews, no dog would bark, from man to animal" (therefore minimizing the alert to the Egyptians of the massive escape). Moshe (Moses) then instructed the Jewish people to feed the dogs all the meats that were left after the exodus.

I was raised with a dog (a wolf) in my Zaidy's (Grandfather's) home in East New York, Brooklyn. My wonderful, spiritual, and learned grandfather taught me the joy of taking care of a dog. I felt adored by human and animal alike, never fearing for my safety or being an only child. My warmest memories of my Zaidy training him in Yiddish commands still makes me laugh. Rewards of cholent marach (marrow) bones were this dog's greatest pleasure as well as walks in the park and snowball fights in the back yard. I am writing a children's book "My Zaidy's Wolf," the adventures of our family's early years in East New York, Brooklyn. I want to tell the story of these fond memories.

My entire family shared the love of dogs throughout the generations. Farfel the poodle, Kugel the Scottish terrier, Romeo the German Shepard, and Dexter the Shitzu are all a part of our canine relatives. Of course, there is my own Lady Cinnamon Babka, the Wheaton Terrier that now lives in Kew Garden Hills. She thoroughly enjoys the company of the dog that belongs to the nice Buckarian family across the street, Oscar the Maltese, and princely Cayenne that guards the marble palace around the corner.

In today's world of fake news, a diseased planet, stress related illness, crippling anxiety, and excessive hatred, is it not comforting to know that with dogs you get absolute approval, endless cuddling, and unconditional love and kisses? Don't we all need that now?

Modesty Shmodesty

I saw her sashaying down the aisle towards me as if she were walking the runway. Her Lady Godiva sheitel (wig) was long enough to trip over, yet she stayed in motion despite her strapless knee length dress carefully zipped over her long sleeved, high neck shell. It was the fact she could walk in her 5-inch, patent Louboutins that impressed me the most.

"Are you the Rebbitzen?" she asked with a twangy Brooklyn accent. "Yes, I am," was the only answer I could think of because I wanted to applaud her performance. "Well, how come you aren't covering your hair?"

I was puzzled given I was wearing a fascinator, orange brocade suit with my gold fabric, jewel-accented, Manolo Blahnik slides. I remained startled and quickly become angry. I blurted out, "Good Shabbos," and immediately walked away. The thought always occurs to me that I should send her a thank you note and floral arrangement because she has served as the source of many lectures about the issue of modesty for me.

How many sins were transgressed during this brief encounter? What does modesty really mean? After all, she was much more adherent to Jewish law. Did she realize what she was doing? I prefer to think that she did not, but the sense of entitlement in her walk and speech told me otherwise. Her brazen, judgmental, singular question also told me how she was raised.

The number of sins that took place in my "Modesty Gate" reached even further than that. She was about 28 and I was old enough to be her mother. Respect for your elders, could be where I stop, but the big stumbling block for me was the public embarrassment she knew she was causing me. This conversation was meant to challenge and chastise me in front of at least 40 people surrounding me. What is the punishment for that sin? Death. Such an act is as if you killed the person because it results in blood being drained from their face. She risked murder by embarrassment to make her point regardless of how it would embarrass me.

The concept of modesty is clearly nothing new. It begins with Genesis and the Garden of Eden. After the sin committed by Adam and Eve, they were faced with the first body covering requirement. What to wear was the first step in the modesty process at the beginning of mankind. The rejection of nudity through shame gives birth to the Torah's (Bible's) idea of covering the body as the means of modesty.

The classical symbol of tzniut (modesty) is the veil. It symbolizes inner and outer privacy, a person apart. Isaiah (3:18) calls it tiferet (glory). The veil was instinctively donned by Rebecca as soon as she observed her future husband in the distance Bareisheis (Genesis 24:65).

That is one reason why the ceremony immediately prior to the chuppah wedding celebration is the bedeken, or the public veiling of the bride by the groom, who includes a blessing for the bride with the ancient words spoken to Rebbeca.

The Jewish dress code has always been influenced by Torah (Bible). Modest clothing is an essential for Jewish women, yet wonderfully interpreted throughout the world. Jewish women tend to wear clothing that is not too bright or form fitting, with sleeves to the elbows, covered necklines, and skirts to the knees. In various Chasidic circles women wear socks, tights, or stockings, as an additional covering.

I marvel at the diversity within the Sephardic sect with their ornate turbans and richly colored head scarves. A stroll down 13th Ave. in Boro Park could rival any runway show during New York Fashion Week. The beautifully dressed women of Crown Heights could recreate the concept of supermodels. Let us not forget the women of the "Five Towns" area that appear to be straight out of the pages of Harper's Bazaar.

Tzniut was intended to preserve the sanctity of the inner human being from assault by the coarseness of daily life. (Psalms 45:14) says kol k'judah bat melekh p'nimah "the whole glory of the daughter of the king is within," however that is followed by the description of her ornately golden and rich attire.

I believe that you need both inner and outer beauty to balance the meaning of modesty within the laws of Judaism. Achieving modesty should be done without losing your individual sense of style.

Nothing modest was practiced the day of my confrontation. On the contrary, more sins were committed in the minutes of that interaction than G-d wishes to witness between any Jewish women.

Here are a few good questions to ask yourself before leaving your home dressed in the latest fashion labels.

Does your skirt that drags to the floor matter if your speech drops people's mouths to the floor?

Does the proper sleeve length protect the length of your disrespectful and improper speech?

Does your tight fitted mid-calf dress lighten up your judgmental stare?

Does your neckline change the bottom line of your sense of entitlement?

To all the fabulous fashionistas of the social media playground and beyond, after you pick out your outfit, pick out your conversation, pick out your public impression, pick out your manners, pick out your self-respect, pick out your sense of dignity, pick out your message to convey to the world. Always remember that who you are on the inside matters much more than how you look on the outside, although it may not come with all the likes you crave.

The Shabbos Table

I must admit that I can be a bit overzealous with my Shabbos table scape. Insisting that each week the table is perfectly coordinated in color scheme, complete with dishes, flowers, silverware and sometimes parsha (scripture) related extras. Almost every week, my husband's son declares that I should become a professional party planner specializing in table scape, because I never repeat a design or a chicken soup recipe.

This whole idea started when I was in my early twenties and thought that my table would certainly overshadow the fact that I had no notion of how to cook. My logical equation was horrible chicken soup + Lenox china x Mikasa stemware = Shabbos.

Throughout the years my creative outlets grew and thankfully I learned to be a better cook.

Shevy Shanik of Shevy Shanik Events is my favorite party planner force of nature to follow on Instagram. Her page is strewn with highly styled editorial pieces in Mishpacha magazine and over the top celebrations. Her sense of style is elegant, yet playful. She transforms a table into a dining experience rivaling Buckingham Palace or High Tea at the Dorchester. Her color choices are reminiscent of a classical painting bordering on the Avant Garde.

I wanted to know more about her role as event planner and how it mixed with her religious values of Shabbos, Yom Tov and faith.

Tobi, "Do you think your gift of creativity is G-d given?"

Shevy, "100% everything I have is from G-d and I thank Him every day for my creativity and being able to channel it to making other people happy."

Tobi, "Is there a reason you feel a special importance for the Shabbos table decor?"

Shevy, "Shabbos is the most special day of the week. The whole week we are leading up to and preparing for Shabbos. The Shabbos and Yom Tov dinner tables should be beautiful and special in every way because they are a reflection on what that holy day is. I have the fondest memories of my parent's Shabbos and Yom Tov tables. The table was always set to perfection with all the traditional delicacies.

Tobi, "Do you need faith in order to deal with your clients?"

Shevy, "Faith is needed in every aspect of my life. I see it a lot with work and that is because in the event planning world as in every aspect of life, nothing goes as planned. You can plan the layout and decor elements of a party for three months only to have to change the layout the day of the event because some furniture did not arrive. There is always plan b, c, and d with many events. I see G-d's hand in every event from start to finish!"

Tobi, "Is there too much importance placed on the table decor and not enough importance given to the purpose of the table?"

Shevy, "Well, I actually love putting together table scapes, so for me there is never too much attention being given to setting your table. It goes without saying that once your table feels special, you will create an ambiance where everyone will be enjoying the party they came to celebrate."

I read an essay from Rabbi Solovetichik about his mother. In "A tribute to the Rebbitzen of Talne Tradition" (vol 17). The words brought tears to my eyes describing his mother's unspoken words on the importance of Shabbos with the living experiences of flavor, scent, sound, and purpose in her preparations. Therefore, this is providing a soul heightened sensitivity to the laws of this holy 24-hour period.

What does the Torah (Bible) have to say further about this special table? It is much more than breaking out your mothers Herend China and your grandmother's silverware. It is all part of a royal presentation for the most important Queen and her escorting angels.

We all invite two angels into our homes every Erev Shabbos, one good and one bad. The Talmud (Shabbat 119a) tells that two angels escort us home from the synagogue on Friday night. When they enter our doors to witness the brilliance of Shabbos reflected in the candles, silver, china, challah, and fragrance of foods, the good angel declares that they should find the same on the following week, and the bad angel must respond "Amen."

If our homes are just the same as every other day, the bad angel wishes the same for the next week and the good angel must respond "Amen." It is about which angel will be a quest at your table that week.

Chabad goes further answering why we sing the Shalom Aleichem hymn at dinner. In this song/poem, we wish these angels peace, we welcome them, we ask them to bless us, and we bid them farewell.

It should be a labor of love for G-d as our guest, that can be seen in every tablecloth, napkin, flatware, stemware, challah cover, and kiddish cup. I suggest you open your china cabinet for it.

Dead Sea

On our bus ride to The Dead Sea, the tour guide promised nothing short of a series of medical miracles. Multiple minerals soaked in the waters for 2000 years can cure almost anything was the better portion of her description of this salty aquatic surprise. Since it was my husband's first trip to Israel, I felt compelled to show him all the tourist highlights of this magnificent country. Having visited the Dead Sea since I was 12, painting myself in mud and floating above a pink rock salt floor, I knew this would be a fun adventure for him. The sea with no fish or life of any kind has grown into a massive industry of cosmetics and other related areas.

One is almost assaulted upon arrival at the airport with advertisements from companies such as AHAVA, PREMIERE, BLACK PEARL and other assorted brands of seemingly magical treatments enhanced with the minerals of this region. The best hair care company using these magic minerals is SAPHIRA. Having had the privilege to know the owners well and watch the rise of the brand, I called one of them for a chat. Rebbetzin Aviva Tessler and her family are immensely proud of their formula, packaging, fragrance, and performance of Saphira.

Tobi, "How has using Dead Sea minerals connected you with your Jewish history?"

Aviva, "Knowing that the Saphira product line is composed of the 26 Dead Sea minerals transports my hair, body and soul to a holy space that has a healing and historical continuum throughout thousands of years. It is interesting to note that there are 26 minerals in the Dead Sea, which is also the gematria for Hashem's (G-d's) name which adds a deeper spiritual significance to the holiness of this space."

Tobi, "Does Saphira (the brand) have a social purpose?"

Aviva, "Saphira, the CEO and Founder, established the 26 mineral product line on the social tenets of Positive Psychology. Saphira implemented an empowerment program with young girls at risk called Strong Women, Strong Girls. Saphira supports giving back such as pop-up salons for children with cancer, empowerment programs such as guiding young girls at risk to design their own shampoo bottles and listing the ingredients they need to get through a day."

Tobi, "How do beauty products fit into your Torah (Bible) values?"

Aviva, "The Saphira metaphorical message is about finding the "minerals" or the beautiful qualities inside each one of us. The Torah teaches us that each person is created with Tzelem Elokim, in the image of G-d. If we can live with that awareness and positive energy, then the opportunities of feeling beautiful within and on the outside is boundless."

Tobi, "Do your products exude faith in yourself as a woman of faith?"

Aviva, "Yes, it is crucial that our surroundings, our choices and the products we use, must send us good energy and make us feel good about ourselves. Everything in our daily lives is a choice. When we make good choices, it reinforces our character, our self-confidence, and the belief in things much bigger than ourselves such as our faith."

Tobi, "How did you transition from Rebbetzin to beauty mogul?"

Aviva, "I like beauty mogul. As a Rebbetzin, I saw myself as a cheerleader (sans mini skirt) for a community of people that I love and wanted them to feel beautiful and special. As a beauty professional I see a similar cheerleading role in wanting each person to feel and look beautiful. Saphira is a professional healing haircare line that promotes beauty that begins inside and is transported outside.

I needed to find the Torah (Bible) significance of these minerals and the special place they derive from.

After all, this salt is related to a place called Sodom. Which would mean that because of the destruction of the most infamous city in the Torah (Bible) came a beauty treatment. Quite odd or poetic.

The parched desert which now houses the Dead Sea or Yam Hamelach was once a fertile plain through which the Jordan River flowed, periodically flooding the entire plain and creating a lush green region."

From the Torah (Bible), we can identify that incredibly evil civilization as Sodom and its sister cities. The Torah (Bible) relays their complete destruction as described in Breishis (Genesis). Even Abraham's prayers on their behalf were ineffective, and "G-d overturned these cities, and the entire plain." The formerly fertile area became a barren, salt-encrusted desert and toxic substances were released from the bowels of the earth. Since the Jordan's waters began to collect in this deep area, it created a large lake with salt and asphalt, where no fish, organisms or plants can live in it therefore naming it the "Dead Sea."

Way before AHAVA, The Egyptian Queen Cleopatra built cosmetic and pharmaceutical factories in the area. Later, the Nabateans extracted asphalt from the Dead Sea and sold it to the Egyptians. The Egyptians used asphalt to embalm their dead. The word "mummy" or mummify derives from the Egyptian word for asphalt.

Herod the Great, built several fortress-like palaces near the Dead Sea, most famously Masada. He created one of the world's first health resorts for himself at the Dead Sea. Ezekiel, the great Prophet in his book of Nevi'im, foretold the day the Dead Sea would become a body of fresh water, and fishermen will spread their nets along its shore. Water will descend from the soon to be rebuilt Holy Temple and flow towards the Dead Sea, and its water will be healed and sweetened. "But by the stream, on its bank from either side, will grow every tree for food; its leaf will not wither, neither will its fruit end; month after month its fruits will ripen, for its waters will emanate from the Sanctuary, and its fruit shall be for food and its leaves for a cure."

According to Chassidic teachings (as described on the Chabad website) the healing of the Dead Sea has an especially important significance. In the Book of Brieshis (Genesis) we are told that on the second day of creation G-d separated the "Upper Waters" and the "Lower Waters." The Midrash tells us that when this occurred, the Lower Waters wept, "We, too, want to be in the King's presence."

Mystically speaking, water is equated to the pleasure principals. There are two versions of pleasures, the "Upper Waters," are the spiritual pleasures for the souls (neshama) and angels that inhabit the upper world. The "Lower Waters," are the earthly humanistic pleasures that exist within the physical world.

The Lower Waters cry that they are restricted to the lowly pleasure of physical bodies that inhabit the lower world. This bitterness expressed by the "Lower Waters" is symbolized by the bitterness of salt water collected of salty tears. Specifically translated to the saltiest of water, the Dead Sea. Perhaps, G-d's division of the two bodies of water was for us to heal the lower with prayers to G-d and observance of His will for His people. Therefore, converting the lower realm tears from salty to sweet. In doing so, hoping to bring the fresh flowing water of Torah (Bible) to all of mankind.

There is a lot to think about while you are afloat like a typical tourist in one of Israel's fun and fascinating attractions, or simply washing your hair.

The Tale of Two Queens

Once upon a time, in the empire of Persia, lived a Queen with a troubling dilemma. Can you imagine her confusion when she was given the message to appear in public naked by her husband? It was a request that went way beyond the emperor's new clothes. Her closets were filled with custom designed haute couture ensembles that the Persian empire's artisans prepared her royal highness. It seemed odd that the King demanded her entrance into the banquet with no clothing at all. After all, it was she that had royal blood and married a mere commoner. Not only did he disrespect her heritage, but he challenged her self-worth. How dare he ask this of her? Has he gone mad with power? She refused again and again until her husband deliberated with his cabinet and decreed death as her punishment.

Queen Vashti died desperately trying to maintain her dignity and honor. We learned as children different evil accounts of the infamous Vashti from her dermatological issues to growing a tail, but we never really saw the first miracle of Purim. Queen Vashti exercised a modesty virtue that Jewish women throughout the ages have practiced. The virtue is Tzniut. Her death is the result of her refusal to act immodestly.

It is said that she was difficult, hateful, and feisty, but her final act was divine. Hashem's (G-d's) first of many miracles was changing her behavior to exit this world with the utmost significance.

The miracles of irrational behavior continue with a beauty pageant. Rather than marry into another royal family to ensure better diplomatic relations, King Achashverosh conducted an extensive search for the most beautiful girl in his kingdom. He filled his Harem with the final selection of women before was winner is found. After a yearlong extensive beauty regime consisting of medicinal oils, complicated diets, personal trainers, and makeup tutorials, the winner was found in little Hadassah, soon to be renamed Esther.

Not only did the King marry a commoner, but a Jewish commoner. It is like watching a crazy Turkish soap opera. Or a Disney classic gone wild. If you start to go into interpretations such as Gemara for a description of Esther, your head begins to spin. It suggests that Esther is 70 years old at the time of her grand coronation. Perhaps there were brilliant plastic surgeons trained especially in massive age reversal. Maybe Persia had the best medical schools on earth. To complicate matters, it is said that Esther's complexion was green. One might ask, how can a 70-year-old woman with Kermit colored skin win a beauty contest in ancient times?

Is Purim the tale of two Queens? One defiant beauty desperately trying to maintain her royal stance. One Jewish woman defying nature and facilitating the continuation of all Jews. There were many superpowers in each of them. Enough to have the Megillah named after one of them. You would think that it would be called Megillah Mordechai, since there are certainly more male components to this story. King Achashverosh, Haman, Mordechai, Haman's 10 sons, and the king's advisors consume a lot of the content. However, the two Queens start the story and give it the happy ending. What do we learn here?

Vashti teaches us the act of divine tzniut and possibly the final act of tshuvah (repentance). Hashem (G-d) orchestrated her Royal Highness of Persia to end her life with the highest virtues, modest behavior. I believe that Hashem's (G-d's) miracle of changing her "normal" behavior was a gift as her modesty decision started the story in motion. Could this story ever have happened if she paraded stark naked at the massive Royal banquet? No, it could not.

As for Hadassah, renamed Esther, we learn about her humility of character, selflessness, and ultimate sacrifice. She was a girl (woman) that would rather have remained Hadassah and not a pageant participant, let alone the winner that became Queen. Her dialogue with her new husband, King Achashverosh, was drenched in respect and modesty. Her unconditional love for her uncle Mordechai was apparent in her strict obeyance of his ongoing instructions. However, her clever orchestration of "parlor meetings" led to a brazen announcement of her heritage. She also acted against her normal behavior to demand the dissolution of a royal decree that ultimately saved all the Jews throughout Persia. Hashem (G-d) rewarded her with a thriving empire and a son or grandson that would finally facilitate the building of the first Bais Hamikdash (Holy Temple). Esther the grandest finale of any tale ever told.

I always found it curious that this holiday (Purim) is when men are permitted an interesting indulgence, they can dress as a woman. Maybe, it is in a respectful nod to the two most interesting, complicated, heroic, and majestic Queens that ever lived.

The Day of Love

Hallmark has not developed the Jewish Valentine's Day of TU B'Av yet. No hearts and xoxo cards or even a Hallmark channel Saturday night movie about the day of love that follows a fast day, in that order. Did you even attempt to bring home a dozen long stem red roses with a box of chocolates? Ok, you are forgiven for this time, but next year, let us explore this day of "amore" a little closer.

The first recorded mention of this date of TU B'Av (15th of AV) is in the Mishnah, it is compiled and edited at the end of the second century, where Rabban Shimon ben Gamliel is quoted saying, "There were no better (happier) days for the people of Israel than the Fifteenth of Av and Yom Kippur, since on these days the daughters of Israel/Jerusalem go out dressed in white and dance in the vineyards. What were they saying? Young man, consider whom you choose (to be your wife)." (Ta'anit, Chapter 4).

The Gemorah finds the origin of this date as an especially joyous day due to a particular social occasion. On this day, the Biblical "tribes of Israel" were permitted to mingle with each other," namely to marry women from other tribes (Talmud, Ta'anit 30b).

Since the holiday starts the night before, its theme takes in the full moon with romance, love, and fertility. Somewhat like an ovulation cycle in monthly charts. The Talmud considers this the greatest festival of the year, with Yom Kippur a close second. That is great importance for a seemingly lightly observed holiday.

Indeed, the 15th of Av is a bit of a mystery. There is no mention of it anywhere in the Shulchan Aruch (Code of Jewish Law), except for the instruction that the tachanun (confession of sins) and similar portions should be omitted from the daily prayers.

Conditional love is addressed in Pirkar Abot, **Ethics of the Fathers**, Chapter 5:16, "Any love that is dependent upon a condition, when the condition ceases; but if it is not dependent upon anything, it will never cease. Which is a love that is dependent upon a condition? The love of Amnon and Tamar. And one that is not dependent upon anything? The love of David and Jonathan."

Love that depends on agenda such as mutual friendship for self-advancement or when a man loves a woman simply for her beauty, have preconditions will never endure. The example of Amnon and Tamar, half siblings of King David, is a twisted example of misguided love for beauty only. However, the love between David and Jonathan, survives royal protocol in the kingdom of King Saul. From this we learn the less superficial version of love.

Only in recent years has this day come to the forefront of Jewish holidays. Israel promotes special festivals of singing and dancing on the night of Tu B'Av to recreate the original social event. Although it had no legal status on the formal Jewish calendar, the beauty, food, and floral companies are working overtime to validate TU B'Av as the Jewish day of ahavah (love). Since Israel has a host of delicious chocolate artisans, shopping for this occasion has become fun. Max Brenner, the famous bald chocolate maker provides gorgeous boxes of delightful truffles and chocolate delicacies.

Stores in Tel Aviv offer "chocolate love for TU BA'v" with Parisian style gift sets or a sampling of their international award winning za'atar pralines. Of course, you can count on Godiva to provide a glorious assortment of chocolate delights. Let us not forget to have the local flower shop deliver the long stem roses just in time to beautify the Shabbos table.

Whatever it is that enhances the romance, TU B'Av is a day wrapped in duality. It sits between the worst part of Jewish history in the first 15 days and the happiest times of love and Shabbos Nachamu. It seems to be the bridge point between sinat chin-um or baseless hatred, for which the holy temple was destroyed, and unconditional love of Tu B'Av and Nachamu. Just like a ballet or an opera, tragedy and ecstasy seem to follow each other. What other way could you fully appreciate love if you did not taste sorrow first?

Whether it is a big box of chocolate champagne truffles, or a bouquet of red roses, or even a heartfelt, "I love you," let us treat each other with love as this is the only sentiment that really matters.

The Magazine Cover

In the alternate universe of fashion magazines, the calendar is months ahead. The September issue is paramount as it is the ultimate celebration, but every cover is a coveted prize. RJ Cutler's famous documentary focused on "Vogue's" Anna Wintour and staff preparing for "The September Issue." It is an interesting documentary about the importance of fashion magazines and the impact they have on the public.

The editor of "British Vogue," Edward Enninful claims, "September issues are important to the fashion world, our largest and most lavish of the year, and a real statement about what the upcoming months will bring." Landing the cover of any month of any fashion magazine is like winning an Academy Award for beauty standards, not to mention a rocket booster to your career.

It has also become a marker in time and a measurement of life going on around us. Vice President, Kamala Harris, made it to the cover with controversy as it did not show respect nor the sense of vitality that she indeed brings to her historic position in our government. It lacked celebratory overtones with wrong color choices, an incorrect outfit and a lackadaisical pose which presented a lackluster attitude toward her achievements.

How does a cover shot reflect our own presentation to G-d? Should we be our best self or do our best to be ourselves? I asked Stephan Rabimov, Fashion Journalist to popular publications, what his thoughts were about this dilemma.

Tobi, "Is the cover an illusion or a goal for women to achieve?"

Stephan, "For some women it can serve as an aspirational moment, for others a total illusion that won't ever be achieved. "Vogue's" September issue is a point of reference for the current state of women's zeitgeist."

Tobi, "Does honesty have anything to do with it?"

Stephan, "No, fantasy is never about honesty. As this magazine sells a fantasy, there is more magic in it than truth."

I am contemplating the duality of these questions as it relates to G-d. Are we required to be perfect and flawless?

"There is nothing as whole as a broken heart," said the Kotsker Rebbe (Hasidic Rabbi, 1787-1859). That statement presents a big crack in the fantasy of perfection that we might imagine G-d wants of us.

The beauty regime begins with the ritual repentance with a goal of a better self. This does not require the impossible standards of a fashion magazine cover. In the Torah (Bible) Portion of Eikev (Deuteronomy), Moses speaks to the people reminding them of them of the countless trials and tribulations they experienced on their journey out of Egypt and in the wilderness. Wandering, stumbling, refocusing, sinning, forgiving, building, and developing their relationship with the Divine was shattered and repaired repeatedly. This message was one of humanity, hope and renewal, not illusions of impossible goals to achieve.

Personal repentance (Tshuvah) means to return, return to your divine truth. It does not mean to return to fantasy expectations. The process of repentance, as laid out by The Ramban (Maimonides), is made up of three stages. They are confession, regret, and a vow not to repeat the misdeed. The true test comes when one finds himself with the opportunity to commit the exact same sin again declines to do so this time.

These exercises enable you to acknowledge and analyze your deeds no matter the depth of quilt or shame. It is a holy way to recognize your flaws at all levels and send you on a path to wholeness.

We are as not perfect as the most beautiful beings, Adam, and Eve. We are not as perfect as the photoshopped, filtered and manipulated magazines. G-d wants us to return to our best selves, our "in G-d's image" selves. That is far more perfect, stunning, and beautiful than any magazine cover could ever be.

Eve Is Not a Woman

Allow me to introduce myself, my name is Hadassah. My uncle Mordechai submitted my application to a beauty contest for the chance of a lifetime to become Queen of Persia, a kingdom that rules over 173 countries. The indoctrination process includes one year of extensive beauty treatments, a special detox diet, and royal etiquette training. Estheticians, nutritionists, and physical trainers promise to transform me from everyday Hadassah to Queen Esther.

However, there is a problem, the glossy brochure for this glorious pageant has no faces of the women on it. How can this be possible? If the megillah (book) of Esther would have played out in 2021, there would be a Queen with no face in view. If this occurred in the USA, she could not be listed as a woman, only a non-binary individual.

It appears that in 2021, Jewish women, and all women, are under attack. However, for Jewish women the extremes are enormous in the religious and secular worlds. The loss of our identity, as Hashem (G-d) designed us, is currently under "reconstruction." Our lives are bombarded with messages of gender fluidity combined with the current definition of the female species, leaving women lost in translation.

Even the government has deleted female words because they tell us it is more "gender inclusive," further digging the grave of the authenticity of G-d's creation. According to the current administration, all uses of gender identification are moot. People need an extra 20 minutes to fill out medical forms due to the countless questions about "how you are, or are not, currently defining yourself."

On the Jewish front, newspapers, publications, and a growing number of Rabbis, no longer allow the faces and sometimes full names of women to be seen. I watched a documentary on Israeli television about this subject recently. What happened in the last fifty years to lead us to this dangerous space, or lack of space? When did the faces of Jewish women become so highly sexualized that they must be forbidden to be seen?

The old Yiddish newspapers of Israel's ultra-orthodox used to publish photos of respected Rebbetzins and women's gatherings. Beautiful and holy women, smartly dressed, posing for a photo. Currently, the same publications will not even print their full names.

How did we evolve into this? When did equal rights turn into a disappearing act of no rights?

In true Torah (Bible) living, any extreme is a playground for disaster. For Jewish women, the stakes are extremely high who we are. This is dangerous by politically and socially robbing the very core of our identities. The twisted and confusing terrain of gender identification defined by the outside world only diminishes us individually, potentially leaving us with no identity at all. In the religious world, our fading images are creating the need to find a safe space to be yourself.

Where do we go?

Are we rearranging the Aishes Chayil (woman of valor) into a faceless creature? Are we over protecting Jewish women by hiding them away?

Recently, I participated in a baby naming ceremony for the granddaughter of childhood friend. As we gathered by Zoom for their (COVID-19 lockdown) party, I started my speech by commending the parents for defying cancel culture and proclaiming the baby a girl. Who would have imagined ten years ago that this would be an issue? What do we want to impart on the next generation of Jewish women?

As I lovingly look at my own daughter heroically comforting me at my bedside, while I recuperate from another demonic round of chemotherapy, I grow more concerned about her future.

Does she know how glorious she is in G-d's eyes? Does she know that her G-d created femininity is highly cherished by her Creator? Does she know the power she has as a Jewish woman? Does she know that no government can cancel her identity to fit into their perverted redefinition of gender?

On the sixth day of G-d's masterful creation of world, He formed the first human out of earth and breathed life into his being. There are several different explanations as to what Eve was created from. The Torah (Bible) declares that she was formed from one of Adam's "tzelas" Bereishit (Genesis) 2:21. The word tzela means "side" as a structural term.

Based on this, many of the commentators understand that Eve was created from Adam's side (one opinion in Bereishit Rabbah 17:8, Rashi 2:21, Ibn Ezra 2:21, Rambam Moreh Nevuchim 2:30, Ralbag 2:21 various commentaries). This follows the opinion in the Talmud (Brachot 61a) that Adam and Eve were initially created as a single being with male and female halves, having both genders fused together. G-d determined that it was "not good" that man be a complete unit should he feel he is perfect and needs no one else, so G-d turned His creation into two incomplete halves (Rashi to Bereishit 2:18). There is also an opinion that tzela means rib (alternate opinion in Bereishit (Genesis), Rabbah 17:8, Onkelos, Targum Yonatan, Chizkuni 2:21, Seforno 2:21 / various commentaries). G-d initially created Adam with an extra rib so it could be used for this purpose (Targum Yonatan, Arbarbanel). There is a third opinion (Talmud Brachot 61a) that Eve was created from a tail or better explained as a tailbone.

On the fifth day, G-d created all the animals male and female. He did not follow through in the creation of woman (Eve), because He foresaw that Adam would complain against her manipulation upon eating forbidden fruit [he would tell G-d angrily Bereishit (Genesis) 3:12: "The woman You put at my side." He therefore waited until Adam requested that she be created. G-d had all the cattle, birds and wild beasts pass before Adam two by two, G-d instructed Adam to name all the species. Adam said, "Each one has a mate, but I do not have a mate?" Once he demanded this with his own mouth, immediately Bereishit (Genesis 2:21), "the Lord G-d cast a deep sleep upon the man and, while he slept [...]" Bereishit (Genesis) Rabbah 17:4. In this midrash, Eve's creation is part of G-d's initial plan of creation.

My favorite in depth explanation of the creation of Adam and Eve comes from the brilliant and innovative mind of Rabbi Soloveichik. In his book, **The Lonely Man of Faith**, he discusses the two versions of Adam 1 and Adam 2. One is a male and female together as a team. The other, a man finding the world too lonely to navigate without a counterpart. I can read this masterpiece repeatedly and still fail to capture the genius in every sentence.

The Rabbis proclaim that Eve was the most beautiful woman ever. To illustrate this, they say that all humans resemble apes in comparison with Sarah's beauty, while Sarah, in turn, looked like an ape in comparison with Eve. Only Adam was handsomer than she, beside whom she, in turn, looked like an ape (Talmud BT Bava Batra 58a). This Midrash has Adam being the most beautiful creature in all the world, since he was created in G-d's image, and directly by Him. Eve was also G-d's handiwork, and therefore no woman was as beautiful as she, even though she was lesser than Adam, for she was a secondary creation, from Adam's body.

Another midrash (biblical exegesis) is about the physical appearance of the woman's body, which differs from that of the man. Bereishit (Genesis) 2:22 states, "And the Lord fashioned the rib," from which the Rabbis learned that Eve was designed as a storehouse (for fruits). Just as a storehouse is narrow at the top and broad at the bottom to hold the fruits, so, too, the woman is narrow above and broad below so that she can bear the fetus (Talmud BT Berakhot 61a). Eve's body structure is presented as functional, for purposes of pregnancy. This explains the different physical structure of man and woman as part of G-d's wisdom in Creation. Each body serves a particular need of its gender. We can also see this in the punishments each received for disobeying G-d's instructions about dwelling in the Garden of Eden. Pains of pregnancy are exclusively female.

Hashem (G-d) created a male and female in almost everything, from linguistics to spiritual plateaus, mitzvot obligations, to valued roles, ceremonial ages, to marriage contracts. G-d had no interest in creating genderless, description less, depiction less, characterization less, portrayal less, specification less, distinction less beings.

What are we teaching the next generation of Jewish women? How are we respecting our mothers and grandmothers that birthed and paved our way?

You can start by never giving in to the new "progressive" nonsensical human definitions. WOMAN, GIRL, FEMALE, SHE, HER, MOTHER,

SISTER, AUNT, WIFE, and GRANDMOTHER are words of power and recognition. They are not meaningless concepts that no longer fit into a progressive ideology. By losing our individuality, we lose our purpose. We did not struggle to obtain women's rights only to be categorized as unmarked specimens. We are the mothers, daughters, and sisters of thousands of generations. We are G-d's design for we were created by Him alone, both male and female. We are the children of our four mothers, Sarah, Rivkah, Rachel and Leah. We are the singers in the dessert with our leader Miriam. We are Shifrahs and Puahs (biblical doulas) that defied Pharaoh and his evil regime to give birth to a nation.

The song still stands as Helen Reddy declared. "I am woman, hear me roar."

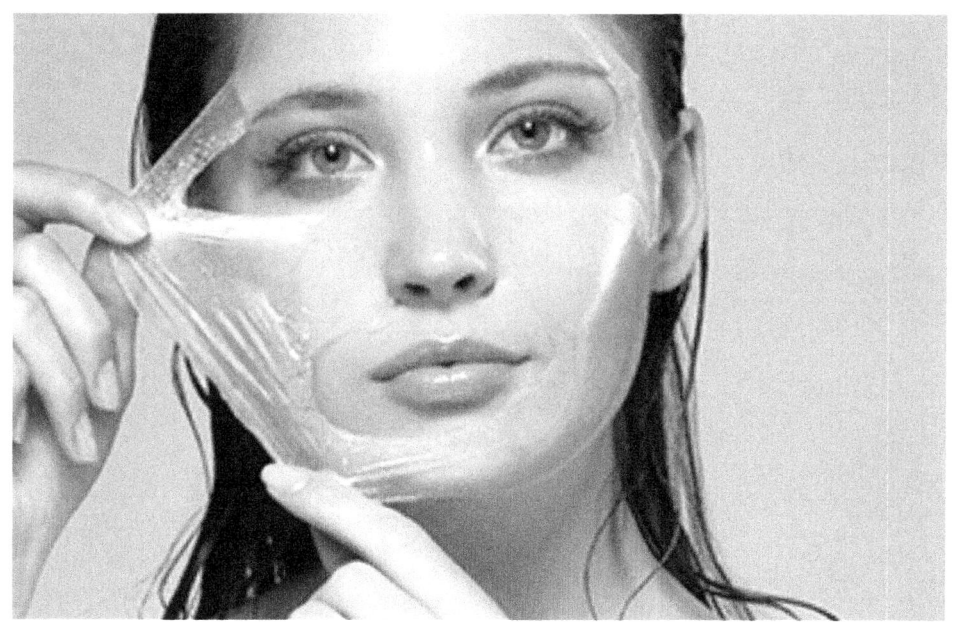

Photo courtesy of Dr. David Shafer

The House of Faith and Fashion

Baccarat Crystal by Tobi Rubinstein

Style & Beauty

Photo courtesy of Tzuri Gueta

Photo courtesy of Aviad Arik Herman

Photo courtesy of Aviad Arik Herman

Photo courtesy of Aviad Arik Herman

Style & Beauty

Tobi Rubinstein by Amy Martin-Friedman

Photos courtesy of Shevy Shanik Events

Style & Beauty

Photo of Tobi Rubinstein

Photo by Tobi Rubinstein

CHAPTER 4

ART

"When I lived in London, I used to visit the National Gallery and my favorite pictures were those of Rembrandt. I really think that Rembrandt was a Tzadik (a saint). Do you know that when I first saw Rembrandt's works, they reminded me of the legend about the creation of light? We are told that when G-d created light it was so strong and pellucid, that one could see from one end of the world to the other, but G-d was afraid that the wicked might abuse it. What did He do? He reserved that light for the righteous when the Messiah should come. But now and then there are great men who are blessed and privileged to see it. I think that Rembrandt was one of them, and the light in his pictures is the very light that was originally created by G-d Almighty,"
written by Rav Abraham Isaac Kook, 7 September 1865 – 1 September 1935) first Ashkenazi Chief Rabbi of British Mandatory Palestine in the Land of Israel. (Reported in Jewish Chronicle, London, September 13, 1935).

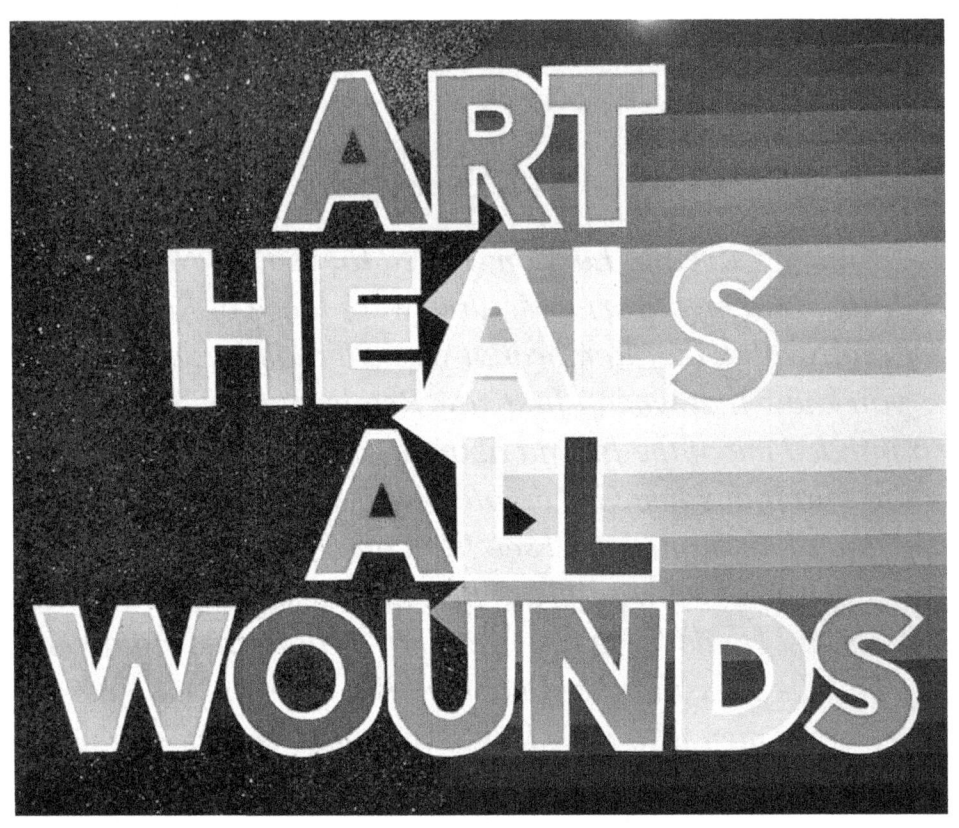

Photo courtesy of Elizabeth Sutton Collection

Counting Sheep

If counting sheep could help you sleep, Menashe Kadishman's sheep can help you see beauty in the animal. The debut appearance of his quirky animals was a live installation of colored sheep at the 1978 Venice Biennale. In 1995, he started painting portraits of sheep, each one different from the next. His instantly recognizable iconic sheep portraits soon became his artistic brand. He was an Israeli artist and sculptor whose artworks are present in many outdoor public locations and galleries all over the world.

"The Akedah" sheep iron sculpture stands in the Tel Aviv University library plaza. My biblical question is, "Why are sheep written about so often in the Torah (Bible)?" The most prominent figures are shepherds. Sheep are involved in holy sacrifice. The people of the nation of Israel are referred to as G-d's sheep.

In the Torah (Bible) chapter of Vayeitzei (Genesis 28:10–32:3), is a jam-packed sheep portion. White sheep, dark sheep, spotted sheep, speckled sheep and sheep with rings around their ankles.

Jacob was greeted by several flocks of sheep gathered by a well. Rachel, one of our four Hebrew mothers, was first discovered shepherding her father's sheep when Jacob fell in love with her at first sight. Jacob became a shepherd for his future father-in-law Leben, hoping to marry Rachel. He amassed great fortune in the sheep commodity which led him back to Israel with his wives and families. He even gifted his estranged brother Esav a huge flock of sheep to avoid a bad ending to a turbulent relationship.

Even kingship plays with sheep as David's life as a shepherd continued to play a role after he left the pasture, slew Goliath, and penned the poetry of the Psalms. "The Lord is my shepherd; I will not want," Psalms 23.

What is with all the sheep? The Midrash (bible commentary) describes our relationship with G-d as Shepherd and we are His sheep.

What does the sheep/shepherd metaphor mean? As a shepherd protects his flock, so G-d protects us. As a shepherd provides green pastures to graze, and G-d provides us with the means to find food and shelter. As sheep, we are devoted to our shepherd and reliant upon Him. Yet, the questionable qualities of sheep are docility and herd mentality. Are we supposed to worship G-d in that manner? Shouldn't we be more like the colorful sheep of Kadishman's paint brush strokes?

The nation of Israel, His sheep, must always be in full recognition of G-d's leadership and greatness with unbreakable loyalty, but not at the expense of individuality. Take the example of prayer. Yes, there are definite laws for the precise time and situations that all Jews must follow the same way, as a herd. Yet, Chassidism teaches the power of Hishtadlus, individual prayer in which one speaks directly to G-d in their own native tongue about their own personal issues.

Women have stretched the boundaries of personal prayer back to 16th century in Eastern Europe. Techines were short prayers, written by and for Jewish women. These extremely popular and targeted prayer books were a woman's conversational holy ritual directly spoken to G-d in Yiddish. They suited everyday religious life and were recited from the kitchen to the mikveh (ritual bath). The best-known author was Sarah bas Tovim, whose booklet known as, "Shloyshah She'orim" (The Three Gates), concentrated on the blessing for the New Moon and the High Holy Days. Having a direct relationship with G-d does not mean that you lack the ability to be part of the herd. Rather, it gives you the ability to balance both collective obedience and personal awareness to G-d's strength and devotion as a shepherd to His herd.

Rebbetzin Miriam Yerushalmi, renown author and speaker, writes in her book **Reaching New Heights Through Prayer and Meditation**, "Try to make G-d a palpable presence in your life through regular meditation and sensitizing yourself to the energy of His presence. G-d should not merely be a mysterious force which we "exalt" and acquiesce to. His life is to be found everywhere if you desire to look for it."

These days a herd mentality could translate to a breeding ground of propaganda and conspiracy theories. Herd immunity could be the cure for this worldwide disease.

As people of faith, we must have belief in our Shepherd we call G-d. We must obey His laws grazing in His pastures of glory and praise His unique qualities. We must herd together as one nation to fight the wolves who prey upon us. We must find our own voice that rises separately from the herd to form our own special relationship with Him.

So, if you are a hot pink sheep, a lime green sheep, or even the black sheep of the family, G-d is your ultimate Shepherd.

The Idols of Social Media

Eyal Assulin and I collaborated on a runway show during New York Fashion Week. He designed a crinoline constructed of elements found in the Israeli Negev desert. This golden structural centerpiece was combined with an embroidered caftan by the Bedouin tribal women of Israel's desert. It was an impactful, emotional, and magnificent presentation to bring attention to Israeli artistry with a focus on the Negev region. Eyal is one of Israel's leading sculptors with highly acclaimed exhibits all over the world including The Haifa Museum of Art.

Assulin (born 1981) lives and works in Ofakim, his childhood town. He graduated from the art department at highly acclaimed Bezalel Academy of Art and Design in Jerusalem. He earned his masters from The Advanced Studies Program at Bezalel. Eyal won the Young Artist prize in 2014 and the Artist in the Community Award for 2010-2014, the only artist who won it for four consecutive years, for his work with local communities in Ofakim and the Bedouin city, Rahat.

For the past 9 years, Eyal has done extraordinary community work by initiating special art projects in the Negev, which is where I met him. He is a lecturer at Sapir College School of Art and Kaye College. Eyal is the creator of the social pilot programs "Creative Place Making & Augmented Reality" in Ofakim and Sderot. These are supported by the Negev coalition and Ness foundation.

His works are reflections of modern society. They speak of current social issues with reference to past cultural stereotypes mixed with biblical resources. He presents grand statements with exceptionally large visuals. From interpretations of ultra-luxury automobiles to distorted construction equipment, Eyal plays with your eyes in scale and design.

His important exhibition "Majesty" introduces a display of "Majestic Escorts," spun out of symbols of ancient Egyptian and current Israeli issues. These are mostly male dominated icons that define masculinity in terms of power, success, and control. Since I have not been to Israel to see his two latest shows, I sent him a series of questions to answer to get a better sense of his overall message.

My questions observed the new "idol worship" of luxury brands and social media which results in distancing ourselves from G-d. The interchange was met with brave and raw answers. Eyal proclaims, "Excess luxury is not the cause of distance from faith, excess luxury is only a byproduct of consumer culture, pop culture, and culture of false wellness. We live in an era of networking and social networks. The absolute truth in the past has been replaced by the multiplicity of different truths and connotations that create various virtual and physical realities in contemporary society." He continues, "Everything that glitters is gold. It must be."

We see social networking figures on Instagram and Facebook, which appear to be happy and abundant. The truth is that these people are busy demonstrating the good life instead of living it. I think that G-d is in every one of us, but contemporary culture attacks us as people and fills us with shells, wrappers, and filters.

Eyal and his works are artistic comments on our own yetzer harah (evil inclination). The pagan ideals of idol worship and multiple G-ds have been modernized with Insta pages, Facebook posts and an excessive drive for fame.

Eyal has hit a sensitive nerve in modern day Judaism. Are we worshipping false G-ds? Are we disobeying one of the first Ten Commandments? We all know the basic instructions of our faith. Are these ideals being trashed with false information, hate and jealousy?

Yes, I am guilty! I have a Facebook, Instagram, and useless Twitter page. Maybe Eyal Assulin's installations challenge us to reckon with the idols of the past, present and future. Are we unaware that political wannabe gods are using social media to manipulate our existence? Why have we made the tech gods rich by our addictions to their devices that track our lives with algorithms? Why have we allowed ourselves to be inundated with garbage? Do we even know the difference anymore?

It seems impossible to fight these Goliaths. We have become conditioned to rely on them for everything, which was their plan. We must find our inner David to slay these giants and do not allow their control over any aspect of our lives. Self-control is our slingshot.

There are countless ways to strengthen your faith with these social media outlets. Torah (Bible) classes, lectures, and prayer services. Gathering online for religious services is a reality now. It is easier than ever to learn in the Digital Age. We must beware of the source of what we read and study today more than ever.

If we use these new sources to focus on our Yetzer Tov (good inclination) and eradicate our Yetzer Harah (evil inclination) then we will be able to discern whether these messages are for good or for evil and choose wisely.

Let us be "followers" of the artist's message, "We are all carry filters that make it hard for us to see our own truth. The truth is G-d dwells within each of us." Think about that when you spend time online.

The Top Banana

Art Basel week 2019 closed in Miami, the only thing on the tip of everyone's tongue was a banana. Specifically, a $120,000 yellow banana duct-taped to a wall, as an art installation by Italian artist, Maurizio Cattelan. Which translated to many bananas and many rolls of tape. The buyers Billy and Beatrice Cox of Miami, FL defended their purchase with a released statement to **The New York Post**, "Page Six" about their acquisition, calling the work "the unicorn of the art world," and comparing it to Andy Warhol's iconic 1962 Campbell's Soup Cans. The couple also intend to loan and eventually donate the artwork to a museum. In an article for **Art News** the couple said, "When we saw the public debate 'Comedian' sparked about art and our society, we decided to purchase it. We bought it to ensure that it would be accessible to the public forever, to fuel debate and provoke thoughts and emotion in a public space in perpetuity."

All this may seem rather "comical" considering the money and attention. Honestly, it could be something straight out of "The Emperor's New Clothes." The tale of a king wearing no clothes as he is publicly praised for the grand clothes he is wearing, until one person has the courage to say, "you are not wearing any clothes, you are naked." Can you imagine if this same king had bananas and duct tape all over his imperial art gallery? Yet, the banana was taken to a totally new level when it was boldly eaten by famed artist David Datuna. David elevated Maurizio's "Comedian" with his live performance peeling, chewing, and swallowing the art in its entirety. After all, isn't G-ds fruit for human consumption? I almost see it as a creative blessing on G-d's foods given to humanity to enjoy.

I was introduced to Datuna's work by a mutual friend from Moscow. I was drawn to his use of assorted pieces of eyeglasses that distort or clarify your vision to really see his subjects of national flags and iconic figures. His accomplishments are serious and quite impressive. His works have been shown in the Smithsonian National Portrait Gallery. For the 2022 World Cup in Qatar, he is planning the largest art installation ever incorporating artificial intelligence. His gallery in Long Island City, NY is home to all his creative expressions of broken sets of China, religious saints and maybe now it will include a fresh produce section! (kidding)

His new collection called 'Box of Lies,' is a colorful display of syringes. He claims it draws from the juxtaposition of the human emotions, fear, and hope. As written on **yrbmag.com**, Datuna said, "Just a bit over a year ago, during my Hungry Artist performance, I said that art is all about the fun it brings to our lives. As 2020 draws to a close, I want to focus on the other aspect of art; it is all about hope, and hope is the key for survival in these challenging times. We fear syringes, but we also fear death, and now a syringe is the ultimate expression of hope. Some see stockpiles of vaccines sitting out there in the Big Pharma warehouses. I see boxes of saved lives." He manages to choreograph a poetic and delicate dance with a bunch of hypodermic needles, as his message is about an alternative state of mind.

I contacted David with a heartfelt "Mazal Tov," on his grand slam public relations move, by eating the banana, knowing full well that he had performed the best thing since the self-shredding 1.4-million-dollar Banksy! I asked him a few questions that I am certain no one ever has. His first response was "I really like your questions!"

Tobi, "Do you believe that your artistic talent is a gift from G-d?"

David, "Absolutely."

Tobi, "How has faith contributed to your work?"

David, "In my opinion, the artist is a representative of G-d on the earth. Therefore, without faith, true artwork cannot be born."

Tobi, "If your works could compose a prayer, what might that sound like?"

He proudly sent me a photo of his Israeli flag paintings.

Tobi, "Your answer is that you have a strong affiliation to the land of Israel? Does that mean your prayer is for peace in Israel, therefore peace in the world?"

David, "Absolutely YES."

Tobi, "Has art become faithless?"

David, "Only in the search could we find something right. Especially in art. It is always a search. Unfortunately, the search is not always true, but the main thing is that in the end we find the right way."

I believe that David Datuna found the truth in his hungry act of art and his continued social consciousness. It is true that art is in the eye of the beholder or vaccinator. It is true that art reflects the times, which are crazy. It is true that art speaks to the generation that is paying top dollar for it. Yet it's most true that only G-d can make a perfect banana.

Dots, A Lot of Dots

One of the Japan's most famous and beloved artists Yayoi Kusama is a mystery of dots. Almost childlike in her appearance and craft, she captures your inner child with playful whimsy.

When she was ten, she began to experience vivid hallucinations which she has described as "dense fields of dots." These imagined images also included talking flowers and fabric patterns. She translated this into art to escape from her overactive mind. She was captured by white stones covering the riverbed which she states as one of her influences for her signature dot restive outlets. Yayoi claims about her self-obsession, "A polka-dot has the form of the sun, which is a symbol of the energy of the whole world and our life, and the form of the moon, which is calm, round, soft, colorful, senseless and unknowing. Polka-dots become movement. Polka dots are a way to infinity."

Her work was the subject of a major retrospective at the Whitney Museum of American Art in New York City in 2012. She brought record crowds to the Hirschhorn Museum and Sculpture Garden in Washington, D.C., in 2017. Kusama's "Infinity Mirrored Rooms" were hugely popular with hundreds of multi angled lights and her polka dot pumpkins. She has a museum dedicated to her work in Tokyo, near her studio and the psychiatric hospital where she has chosen to reside. I look forward to seeing her variety of installations throughout 250 acres of the New York Botanical Gardens. She is debuting her first ever greenhouse installation with new and exciting sculptures.

Who could imagine that a simple dot could hold such meaning in a person's mind and artistic creation? Are dots really that simple?

The Torah (Bible) does not think so. As a matter of fact, dots can alter a meaning behind an entire sentence. They can completely change a sound pronouncement of a Hebrew letter. They can change everything you thought it meant. These dots are significant as they concern an odd placement of printed points preserved in the Torah (Bible). To appreciate these dots, you need to return to the actual Hebrew text in which the Torah (Bible) was originally written.

Hebrew is a beautiful language, but because it is in the Semitic family of tongues, it is markedly different than English. It does not require complete vowel markers to be read. In fact, the Hebrew alphabet is typically considered not have true vowel letters, even though vowels certainly are employed in pronouncing the Hebrew language. This detail makes for a unique reading experience. There is a system of vowel marks added to the Hebrew text to aid the reader in properly identifying the words. They are constructed of dots and dashes that are placed above or below the letters, which allows the reader to pronounce the terms written with precision, for accurate reading comprehension. These vowel markings have faithfully preserved the general pronunciation of the ancient Hebrew text for us. The Hebrew name for these marks is Nikkudoth/Nikudos. While texts with vowel-points can be used in Hebrew books, it is strictly forbidden in an actual scroll of the

Torah (Bible). A person must know how to accurately pronounce the text, or they might easily make a mistake (and will be publicly corrected).

A Sofer (scribe) who writes a Torah (Bible) parchment is commanded to include dots in extremely specific places. The dots are placed above a letter always and are inked to clearly distinguish them as intentional rather than a slip of the feather. These dots are also referred to as Nikkudot but have a more compelling significance than common Hebrew pronunciation. One famous example occurs with the most dots appearing in a Parsha, the book of Devorim (Deuteronomy). The phrase lanu ulevaneynu ad (for us and for our sons unto) has niqqudot over every single letter except for the last letter of the word ad. The reason for the strange use of dots comes from the Talmud Bavli, tractate Sanhedrin 43b. "Why is the dot over lanu ulebanenu, and over the Ayin that is in ad? To teach that He did not punish for the secret (sins) until Yisra'El (Israel) crossed the Yordan (Jordan). These are the words of Rav Y'hudah. Rav NekhemYah to him: "And did He ever punish [all] for secret [sins]? Does it not say, 'unto everlasting?' But as He did not punish concerning secret (sins), so He did not punish concerning that which is revealed until Yisra'El crossed the Yordan."

Dots are hugely significant in their placement all over the Torah (Bible). I do not have the ability to understand why they are positioned where they are. I leave that to the great Torah (Bible) scholars throughout the centuries.

As an artistic expression steeped in emotional pain or multitude of impressions by a sofer's (scribe's) quill, dots have a powerful message for us. Maybe it is a lesson to never underestimate the smaller things in life. Maybe it is a reminder that your small choices are important because they allow you to make the bigger ones, but maybe G-d is telling you that the small mitzvot are just as important as the big ones.

Find your personal dot, understand its worth, big and small, pronounced or silent, simple or complicated, and create your own masterpiece.

An Artist Grows in Brooklyn

If you are a fan of Netflix's "Shtisel," you can't help but recognize the main character of "Kiva" in the real life Zalman Glauber. However, if you did not binge watch the show, let me familiarize you with the plot. The TV series is a melodrama surrounding a Chassidish family living in B'nai Brak with all the restrictions, problems, happiness, devastations, lost dreams, and betrayal as any family. Handsome and uber talented Kiva is a lovesick artist with a turbulent relationship with his father, and his artistic expression. The show gives the viewer a glimpse into the world of strict laws within the tight community in Israel.

Zalman Glauber was born and raised in a tight-knit Hassidic community in Brooklyn, NY with little exposure to art other than paintings of grand Rebbes. His entry into exploring art was attempting to make Sukkot (holiday) paper decorations. He soon developed his craft with elaborate panoramic scenes that took months to prepare. At 18, when his community was "shidduch (arranged marriage) ready," he decided to attend Baruch College where he received his BA. Sensing a need to develop and advance his artistic skills, he asked his Rabbi if he could learn how to sculpt. With permission and instruction on Halacha (Jewish law) he studied with renowned sculptors and found his own artistic expression which lovingly glorifies acts of Judaism.

Does Art belong in this kind of restrictive world? The two seem to clash with judgment and mistrust, or do they? I asked Zalman how he balances it all.

Tobi, "How has faith impacted your art? Some pieces are obvious, and some are not."

Zalman, "Faith is the foundation of my life and upbringing. So naturally everything I do will be impacted by it. Maybe losing my father at a young age (14), was one of many things that strengthened my faith. As long as I can remember I had a strong pull to study Jewish history (tenach). So,

I would say that most of my art would be connected to that foundation. Some pieces are more from a philosophical nature, contemplating the hard questions of life, and its meaning."

Tobi, "How do you handle the fact that art is not a staple in religious homes?"

Zalman, "I think if we go back in time, art was a big part of our existence. Since we can see it says in the Torah, Hashem sent Moshe (Moses) to Betzalel, to help in building the mishkan (tabernacle) and its values. Where the artifacts and the perowches (curtains) were magnificent pieces of art. Unfortunately, during goles (exile), the Jewish people did not have a home, and did not live in one place for long. So, without a place, security, richness, and abundance, there was little opportunity or possibility for collecting and enjoying the fine arts. It is interesting to note that in the time of the Bais Hamigdash (Temple) the Leviyim (priests) were in charge with the art of music and song, a form of art that has never been ripped apart from our tribe. We sing during prayers and Shabbos seuda, hence maybe this is a type of art that was not hard to travel with when we were exiled from place to place. Not long after the printing press was invented, hundreds of years ago, a beautiful pesach hagoda with lots of beautiful art and illustrations was printed. And of course, decorating the sukkah is not new. But today B'H' in America, Israel and different parts of the world Jews live and prosper, and as time goes on, I think more and more people will enjoy Art with a Jewish gefeel (feeling)."

Tobi, "Do you appeal to collectors outside of the Jewish community?"

Zalman, "I cannot dictate where my art will end up. I only hope and wish for it to be in a home where it can touch people in a positive and meaningful way."

Tobi, "Was your creative talent a natural gift from Hashem (G-d)?"

Zalman, "I think each one of us has the divine spark. So, everything we do comes naturally from Hashem. We are made by the creator, to be creative, everyone in their own way. The creativity, and ideas I feel come from above. Technicality, and to perfect the art takes some practice. For some people it is natural and easier to learn. In my case I learned and am still learning art (professionally) for the past 8 years. I cannot say it came easy. Hard work and consistency, and learning to enjoying the journey, are some of the things I learned along the way."

Tobi, "If your art could compose a prayer, what would that sound like?"

Zalman, "Hashem gather all the lost Jews, from all four corners of the Earth, and return us to our home, where you will dwell amongst us 'bim hairu biyumani'."

For the artist, art is a vital expression of self whose talent is given to the Neshama (soul) by G-d Himself. It is a gift, calling and purpose that must be utilized to lead a life of fulfillment.

I believe that Rav Kook said it most brilliantly "Literature, painting, and sculpting are able to bring to fruition all the spiritual concepts engraved in the depths of the human spirit, and so long as one brush is missing, which is stored away in the depths of the spirit, which ponders and feels, but has not been realized, there is still an obligation on the purposeful work to realize it."

A Colorful Life

When you walked into her studio in Long Island City, you were transported back to your childhood. Bursting in color and sparkling in glitter, it is a world of joy, hope, and love. She has since moved to Miami, setting up another environment of creativity as only she can do. Elizabeth Sutton is a self-taught artistic machine. Her comfort zone lies between butterfly dreams and the end of a rainbow. Elizabeth Sutton Collection is a brand and a movement of survival through art, creativity, and design. Her personality immeasurably draws you into her world of expertly executed linear murals, strong message panels, color coded landscapes, brand logo products, and ambitious collaborations.

I knew I could relate to her on many levels, especially spiritually. Being an artist myself, I found my happy place in every painting that hung on the walls of her studio. It brought memories of Crayola boxes, paint kits, brushes, and canvases that saved me during difficult times in my childhood as well as the challenging adult times. Among many works, "Art Heals all Wounds" and "Blessing in Disguise" are two of Elizabeth's paintings that tell her story.

After some unfortunate circumstances, Elizabeth picked up her paintbrush and built an empire in a short time. A-List celebrities such Kylie Jenner and Andrea Botticelli have collected her original art. Collaborations with Joe & The Juice and Jankovic made her a mega brand superstar with building size murals of her work around NYC.

Miami has produced many more outlets in furniture design, tile, jewelry, and carpets. You may have taken a photo in front of her bull mural at the Wall Street Grill or sipped your drink by her art at the DoMa gallery. You could have walked past her painting at the Eden Roc Hotel, St Barts. She does not plan on stopping and I am happy and proud of her success.

She honors her career with excellence in her craft. The press adores her, and she is often covered in the "Wall Street Journal," "Architectural Digest," "The New York Times," and "Forbes." She has become an artistic explosion heard across the intersections of art, design, fashion, home décor. and architecture. Her clients and social media admire and relate to her positive force.

Elizabeth's mastery of color is a spiritual journey. I knew what I would ask her had to be thoughtful, insightful, and truthful.

Tobi, "Do you believe your artistic talent is G-d given?"

Elizabeth, "I believe that everything in life is G-d-given, especially innate talent. I never studied art, never took an art class, and I never study color theory. My career developed out of necessity, hard work, and now I am realizing pain. I am self-driven and work incredibly hard, but I certainly believe that I was blessed with many creative talents. These talents were granted to me from G-d, for which I'm incredibly grateful."

Tobi, "Does your art reflect what G-d has given you?"

Elizabeth, "My art reflects my life experiences, and my process is definitely a path to heal from challenging obstacles I've been through. Growing up religious, I have always been a faithful person, and have continued that spirituality into my adulthood. I express gratitude and pray daily. I believe that all the obstacles put in my way were put there by G-d to give me strength and the capacity to get through life with a positive perspective."

Tobi, "Is there a place in the art world for true faith or fake faith?"

Elizabeth, "I hate to say it because I'll get shunned, but I personally feel that much of the art world is fake. I am not sure that the concept of faith is ingrained within the world of the arts. Ironically, I find the nature of the bureaucracy behind the gallery and museum fine art world to lack authenticity and uniqueness. It creates an expectation for people to follow certain paths, and not necessarily focus on talent. I personally don't find that faith is attached to the art world, but I am certain that individuals within the art world are faithful themselves."

Tobi, "Do you need faith to be in the current art arena?"

Elizabeth, "I feel as though faith is a personal choice that is particular to the individual and not tied to an industry. There are both faithful and nonfaithful people in all industries. However, I do find that many artists have some sort of belief. This is a generalization, but creatives who follow their passion are often making some type of statement whether it be related to politics, society, faith, or culture. I do not want to label the industry, so all I can say is that it personally plays a role in my life, in my art, and in my capabilities as a mother and human being. I don't think I'd be able to get through anything without having a strong sense of spirituality and faith that G-d is watching over me, my family, and is always protecting us."

Tobi, "If your art could compose a prayer what might it look like?"

Elizabeth, "My dear spiritual advisor, friend, and mentor Tobi Rubinstein got me on a path to lighting my Shabbat candles every Friday, no ifs, and, or buts. The next artwork that I would love to create in the arena of faith is a painting of a photograph of a woman lighting her Shabbat candles. This tradition has taken on special meaning to me. I light my candles alongside my two incredible children, and during these moments I express gratitude to G-d for blessing me with my many talents, with my strength, with my intelligence, with my health, and with my family. I ask G-d to protect and watch over all those that I care about. I ask G-d to give me the strength to become a better person and take away any sort of evil that may live inside me and give me the strength to get through any obstacles in my way. I would like the painting of a woman lighting Shabbat candles to evoke feelings and sentiments of strength, family, love, support, gratitude, and a strong belief in G-d."

Where does color fit into Judaism? The message of color is seen throughout the Torah (Bible). Joseph's brightly colored coat provoked jealousy and outrage from his brothers. The ashes of red unblemished heifers provided the ultimate ritual cleansing. The precise shade of techilis blue needed was woven into the costume worn by the high priest in the Holy Temple. The rainbow of colors after a rainstorm is the promise from G-d to never repeat worldly destruction as He did in the time of Noah and the flood.

However, I find the most in-depth reality of color in Kabbalistic teachings. The correspondence between the Divine Emanations/Sefirot, and their associated colors, taught by Rabbi Joseph Tzayach (c. 1500 C.E.), explored and explained further by Rabbi Moshe Cordovero (author of the "Code of Jewish Law") in his book **Pardes Rimonim**.

The Divine Sefirot and their allegorical colors are as follows:

1. Crown/Keter – A blinding invisible light.

The Sefirot of Intellect:

2. Wisdom/Chokhmah – Includes all colors.

3. Understanding/Binah – Yellow and Green.

The 7 Sefirot of Emotion (emanations):

4. Loving kindness/Chesed – White and Silver.

5. Strength/Judgement/Restraint/Gevurah – Red and Gold.

6. Beauty/Mercy/Tiferes – Yellow and Violet.

7. Eternity/Victory/Netzakh – Light Pink.

8. Splendor/Humility/Hod – Dark Pink.

9. Foundation/Connection/Yesod – Orange.

10. Sovereignty/Malchus – Blue.

There is an interesting Jewish monthly chart reflecting traits through colors and the original twelve tribes of Israel:

1. The month of Tishrei is purple for the tribe of Efrayim with attributes on touch, foundation, and proof.

2. The month of Chesvan is deeper purple for the tribe of Menasha with attributes on loving kindness and smell.

3. The month of Kislev is light royal blue for Binyamin with attributes of sleep.

4. The month of Tevet is darker royal blue for the tribe of Dan with attributes of anger.

5. The month of Shevat is teal blue for the tribe of Asher with attributes of eating.

6. The month of Adar is lime green for the tribe of Naftali with attributes of laughter.

7. The month of Nisan is darker lime green for the tribe of Yehudah that attributes faith and speech.

8. The month of Iyar is yellow for the tribe of Yisaskar with attributes of understanding, joy and thought.

9. The month of Sivan is gold for the tribe of Zebulon with attributes of progress, acknowledgment, and sincerity.

10. The month of Tammuz is orange for the tribe of Reuben with attributes of might and awe.

11. The month of Av is orange red for the tribe of Shimon with attributes of kingdom, and lowliness.

12. The month of Elul is red for the tribe of Gad and attributes beauty, mercy, and action.

13. The month of Adar Sheni is black to grey for the tribe of Levi with attributes of knowledge and unification.

Color and the use of color is a deep mediation with each shade created by G-d in Breishis (Genesis) in the creation of each day. G-d created color to be used in many different circumstances, yet for Elizabeth Sutton, the emotions of color with different hues are in all aspects of her life and business.

Tobi, "How has the pandemic changed you and your art?"

Elizabeth, "It has definitely made me more resilient and adaptable to change. I restructured my entire business and moved my family and business to a new city which was a major life shift and not an easy decision to make. But as someone who thrives on inspiration, New York had become a highly uninspiring place to be, and I knew that for the sake of both me and my children's mental health I needed to make the move.

Everything in life is about attitude, perspective, and how we view things. I feel that COVID-19 was a blessing for me and my family. I put a lot of structure in place in my business and got to spend the extra time with my kids. I definitely feel as though people can now relate more to certain artworks that were inspired by loss and traumas, as almost everyone in the world has just gone through a trauma whether they feel it ended up being a positive or negative."

My hope for everyone to learn from her is that the palette and path of your own individual life will connect you to the colorful moments that G-d has blessed you with, no matter how uncolorful you feel at times of distress, challenge, turmoil, and doubt. Turn yourself around to see the beautiful colors in yourself and others.

Photos courtesy of Eyal Assulin

Art

Tobi Rubinstein courtesy of the David Datuna App

The House of Faith and Fashion

Photo courtesy of Zalman Glauber

Art

Photo courtesy Elizabeth Sutton Collection

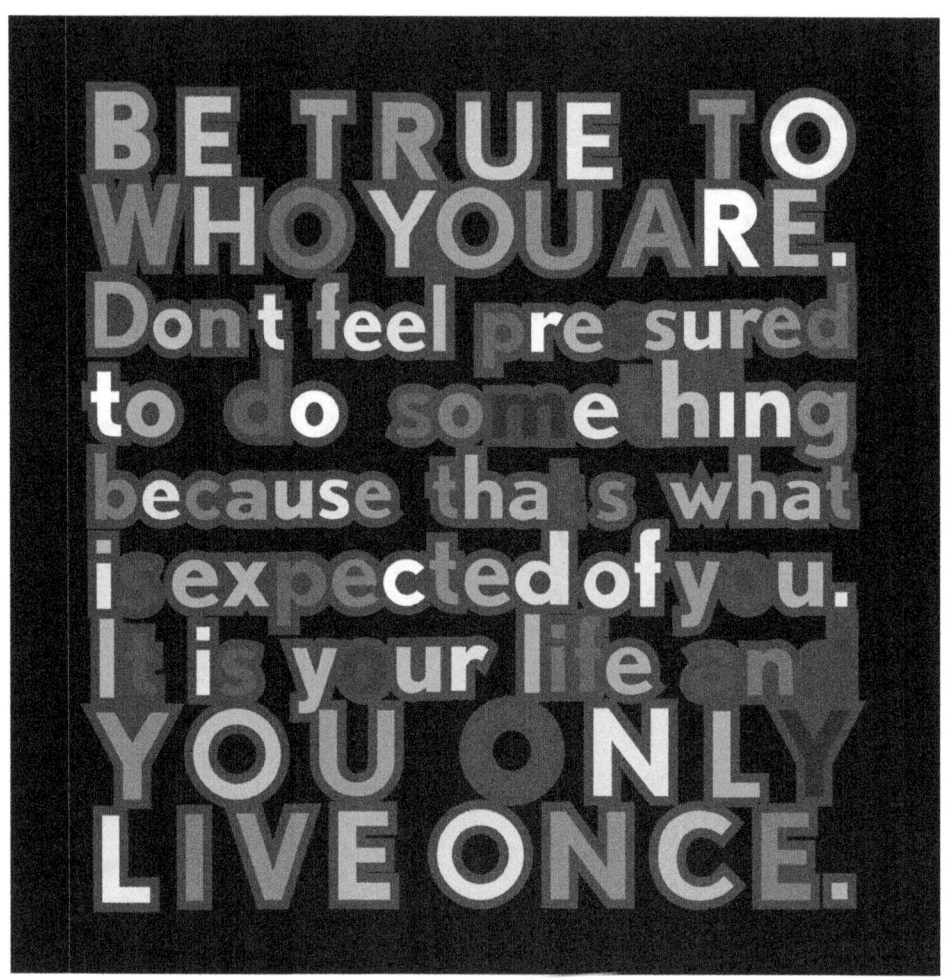

Photo courtesy Elizabeth Sutton Collection

Art

Photo courtesy Elizabeth Sutton Collection

The House of Faith and Fashion

Painting by Tobi Rubinstein

Art

Painting by Tobi Rubinstein

Painting by Tobi Rubinstein

Painting by Lola Rubinstein

CHAPTER 5
INFLUENCERS

"Make your Torah a permanent thing. Speak little and do much. And receive every person with a cheerful countenance."
Ethics of The Fathers (1:15)

Influencers

Fathers Matter

Although I cannot pretend that I have always gotten along with my late father, I certainly learned some powerful life lessons from him. My dad, Abe Roth (ZL) was a strong presence in the community, with an impeccable work ethic that remains unmatched to this day. Abe Roth, the master plumber, and owner of A Roth Plumbing and Heating was a larger-than-life personality and a brand unto himself. People still tell me stories about their broken hot water heaters, busted pipes, and countless bathroom renovations that he repaired, rearranged, and resurrected for them, all while balancing a cigar and a wrench. All of their touching stories end with the same sentiment, "Your dad was the greatest and most honest plumber. We miss him." In that respect I shall remain known as "The Plumber's Daughter," an exceptionally good title for my next book.

As his only child, I learned extensively about craftsmanship and creativity, because my father was meticulous about connecting shape, form, and color. This probably jump-started me into the creative process of fashion and design. I have a timely and unexpected story to share that is as relevant today as it was the day it happened.

My grandparents, Mechel and Tova Roth, left Poland and immigrated to the United States the late 1920s. Arriving as a newly married couple with the hope of thriving in the "Goldene Medina," (golden land). As many families arrived with children to feed and bills to pay, the economy in the US crashed to nothing. "The Great Depression" of the 1930s brought desperation and grave hardships to most of its citizens. Endless bread lines were how they received food from government assistance. It was the longest, deepest, and most widespread depression of the 20th century.

My Zaidy (grandfather) and his family traveled wherever there was work for himself as a carpenter. Of all the unlikely places, they moved to Mobile, AL, in the "Deep South." My father was about 10 years old then and my uncle Chaim was 8. They had 5 or 6 other siblings that included my aunts Cynthia and Bella Rabinowitz.

The stories my father told me of his adventures there were of their makeshift yeshiva (Hebrew school) where he taught his younger siblings Torah (Bible) in an abandoned treehouse. He delivered these stories with a thick southern accent to create the correct tone, and I would laugh each time I heard them. As a child I imagined how wonderful it must have been to have such freedom without teachers or real classrooms.

One day, when I was about 10 years old, I participated in a terrible childish stunt with my friends from my block in Queens, orchestrated by the neighborhood bully against an innocent black lady. As she elegantly strolled down our block on 76th Road, we started making fun of her like little monsters. She ran away from us as she approached the Main Street.

My father witnessed this encounter from the screen door and stormed out to grab me by my dress and drag me home with an expression of anger that I will never forget. He forced me to sit on the couch and proceeded to teach me a lesson that changed my life. He screamed, "Toba Leah, let me tell you the rest of the story about living in Mobile, AL.

There were signs everywhere that said, "No Negros, No Jews and No Dogs!" He told me about the lynchings and beatings he witnessed. The White cultural hatred of Blacks and Jews caused them to be treated no better than common animals. Jews could not even use the same bathroom as Whites. The multiple times that he and his brothers were beaten up because they were Jewish were horrific. Then came the punch line that I will never forget, "So Toba Leah, do you think you are any better than that lady that you frightened today? DO NOT forget who you are!" That day I experienced so much scorn and punishment from my father, and I felt his grave disappointment in me. He knew that I would never view Blacks or any minority in the same light again.

It is not every day that a Jewish orthodox girl receives a lesson like this about racism and antisemitism in the USA. In our communities, the lesson is more commonly about antisemitism as it relates to the Holocaust.

At a time of great unrest in our country between races, genders, politics, and power, I choose my slogan, "Fathers Matter." It is what they teach you to respect that matters. It is what they teach you to love that matters. It is what they teach you to do that matters.

I am proud to say that my father taught me very well. I have shared my life's joyful and sorrowful events with brilliant and faithful black men and women as well as with those of other faiths, races, and political views. I have developed businesses, shared Shabbos (Sabbath dinners), cried, laughed, danced, cooked, created, and traveled with the best crew of people I could have ever known because of my father's wisdom.

Pirkai Avot says, "Who is smart? One that learns from others."

I, the plumber's daughter, have learned a valuable lesson from my Dad about what really matters and how to treat others.

The Book of Ruth

While it might not be the most dramatic of biblical stories, the Book of Ruth has an interesting variety of characters and fates that relate to any modern-day literature. There are Ruth-like scenarios from the original story that are rearranged to form a new story drawing from the original's plot. In the timeless book, there are raw emotional circumstances that seem very current, such as loss of life, money, social status, and the humiliation of falling from grace. You are following a princess to a pauper, a matriarch to a malnourished, the death of family to the birth of Moshiach (Messiah).

It is the story of unnatural family members that leads to a highly unusual relationship between a mother-in-law and daughter-in-law. It moves past mutual grief to eternal devotion. In the book, we are informed that the once Grande dame of Israel, Naomi has lost her husband and sons in their move to Moab, leaving her poor with two ex-princesses who are her daughters-in-law, Ruth and Orpah. That is all that remains of a once prominent family.

It is Ruth who chooses to cling to her mother-in-law despite that common sense would dictate otherwise. These are her famous and haunting words from the text; "Entreat me not to leave you, or to return from following after you. For wherever you go, I will go. Wherever you lodge, I will lodge. Your people shall be my people, and your G-d my G-d. Where you die, I will die; and there will I be buried."

These words speak loudly and very personally to me because I am blessed with the great story of my own mother-in-law.

My biological mother abandoned me after my parent's explosive divorce when I was just eighteen. She left me a scribbled note on our kitchen table as her goodbye, and I have had extremely limited and painful contact with her since. To compensate at that young age, I created a fantasy of the mother I wished for to sooth the reality I survived. Starting from age twelve, I struggled in my relationship with her, never understanding how G-d chose this mother for me. Today, I have released the anger, replacing it with forgiveness, which opened a new path to realizing my self-worth. I will leave the story right here.

Thirty years later, I met Donna Schneier and I later became her daughter-in-law. Unfortunately, the marriage to her son ended badly, but the Ruth-like story began in its place. Since my public divorce took a hard toll on me, it was Donna that nursed me back to life. She took charge of her position as mom, therapist, and fairy godmother, making sure that every detail of my life came back together after it was broken to pieces.

She taught me the true meaning of courage, self-worth and perhaps most important of all, unconditional love. She became my Mama Donna. Like Naomi, she taught me how to start over with dignity, even when everything precious has been taken away from you.

Like Naomi, she provided me matriarchal strength in the worst of times and in the best of times. Like Naomi, she was practical, calculating and encouraging when I was finding a Boaz (again). Like Ruth, I clung to every word and the advice she gave me, because I knew that she had my best interest in mind. Like Ruth, I knew I had only loss behind me and love in front of me no matter what the circumstances would be. Like Ruth, I was certain she could reshape my future.

As a child, I used to close my eyes and wish hard enough for a different mommy, I probably manifested Donna's arrival as an early exercise of, **The Secret**. To me, she is the most stylish, spectacular, creative creature I have ever met. She taught me the appreciation, significance and value of creativity, craftsmanship, love, and truth in art, as well as life.

Donna Schneier is a worldwide force in art jewelry. Her personal collection was gifted to the Metropolitan Museum of Art several years ago with a perfectly curated exhibit of her own. She began collecting post-World War II international jewelry in the mid-1980s, beginning with pieces by artists such as Robert Ebendorf and Otto Kunzli, and since then continued to collect museum-quality works. Her passion for art jewelry has transformed the importance of the category in major museums around the world. She continues to nurture, inspire, collect, and sell jewelry from designers that push the boundaries of materials, scope, texture, and message. Her elegant style is seen in everything she does in home decor, table spaces, cooking and wardrobe. She enhanced everything I thought I knew. I bow to her taste level and applaud her influence in my life. She is a gift to me.

It is funny when I read about the natural hate between a mother-in-law and daughter-in-law in the Gemorah (Yevamot and Shabbos). I struggle with the biblical Mitzvah of Kibud Am, honor your mother. I realize that it is complicated because I am her ex-daughter-in-law and she is my ex-mother-in-law. G-d, in His infinite wisdom, has untwisted what was a harmful maternal chain of events into a straight line of connection and happiness with Mama Donna.

I realize that it is an unbelievable story, so I'll just let Mama Donna explain it in her own words, "In keeping with the story of Ruth and Naomi, a favorite of Jews by choice, I have been blessed with a daughter by choice, my daughter-in-law Tobi, who has stood with me, sharing life with all its joys and sorrows. From sadness, a Phoenix arose to brighten my years," Donna Schneier.

Love Is the Cure

It has been over two years since my Uncle Chaim Roth (ZL) passed away and I gave a dvar (talk) Torah (Bible) on his Yurzeit (Memorial Day). I am certain many of you know of my dear uncle as he was the founder of H Roth Adjusters. Sometimes I feel like my entire family services the Jewish neighborhoods, since my wonderful first cousin Aryeh (Archie) Rabinowitz builds and repairs homes with his company, All Boro Group, and his son David takes care of the yards and flowers with Elegant Lawns & Landscaping.

I can tell you with that I love my family unconditionally and that is the purpose of this essay.

Since my father and uncles were all Kohanim (priestly class), I addressed the issue of the Priesthood as discussed in the Torah (Bible). G-d gifts the priesthood to a select few with great responsibilities included in their sacred jobs. Yet, all but one chore cannot be done since there is no Bais Hamikdash (Holy Temple) standing today. There are no duties of sacrifice or service, only Bircat Hakohanim (blessing of the priests) have survived until this day. I had this lively discussion with my father, Abe Roth, by his hospital bed, posing a question to him that he could not answer. Why, of all the blessings in the world, does the blessing of Kohanim end in the word AHAVAH (love)?

The Lakewood Mashgiach, Rav Matisyahu Solomon Shlita explains, "It is in fact the need for that love that requires their responsibility be decreed from on High. Their task is not to merely bless the congregation, they must bless them with sincere, genuine, unadulterated love."

To utter the three short verses of Birkat Kohanim should be so simple, but it is not. It is only a handful of words. Easy words, but words made heavy by the command that they be delivered with genuine unconditional love. It is love that makes the task so challenging. The Kohanim needed G-d to issue a decree they perform their blessing in such an emotional manner.

The big question is why is it so hard to bestow genuine blessings of love? Is it that hard to love another Jew, another family member, another child, or another friend? Yes. It is so difficult and imperative that Rabbi Akiva taught that v'ahavta l'reiach kamocha, loving your fellow man as you love yourself, is foundational for all Torah (Bible).

It is contrasting personalities that makes this even more complicated. Kohanim have a tendency toward anger, or in modern day terms, "anger management issues." It is clearly explained in the Gemorah Shabbos Daf yomi Daf 149. What a juxtaposition G-d put the Kohanim in.

I can attest to these contrary characteristics within my own family. However, my Uncle Chaim mastered these divine dualities with great ease. Although he had a tendency towards anger, his love was also expressly freely. He had the love of a Kohen Gadol (high priest). I know there were times when he saved me. I know there were times when he was deeply disappointed in me. More importantly, I knew that he loved me. He possessed the great wisdom of knowing when to be encouraging and when to be reprimanding, as if he already knew the outcome.

It was certainly not a coincidence that the seudah fell on Tu Bav, Judaism's day of love, the happiest day of the year and a holiday matched only in significance by Yom Kippur.
The day and the man brought me to tears as the world today is so full of hate, it is almost inescapable. Why can't we love one another?

Today it seems harder than ever. However, maybe that is the message that G-d is sending. The example of the Kohen is really a reflection of our current state. We are filled with anger and fear of what surrounds us politically, socially, economically, and spiritually. Yet, just as the Kohen, G-d commands us to love one another even under these hostile conditions.

Here are a few reminders of what love is and is not.

Love is about imperfections that are appreciated no matter what.
Love is about respecting one another no matter what.
Love is about sacrifice no matter what.
Love is about family no matter what.
Love is about your fellow man, no matter what.

Love is not about perfection.
Love is not about self.
Love is not about agenda.
Love is not about being right.
Love is not about opinions.
Love is not about being a victim.

That is the mantra that my Uncle Chaim Roth, who was a father, brother, Zaidy (grandfather), uncle, husband, and great Zaidy wanted to leave as his legacy. Being a Kohen is hard, being loved by a Kohen makes life much easier.

Fran The Magnificent

There are certain women that you meet in life that make an everlasting impression. You might even refer to them as iconic, perfect profiles for personal mentors or subjects of a book. Fran Laufer (ZL) was most definitely one of those figures. She encompassed all the best characteristics of a Jewish woman, or in Yiddish terms "ala maiylus." She was as Katy Perry sings "cause baby, you're a firework, come on, show 'em what you're worth."

I first encountered her when I was honored at her annual Bikur Cholim luncheon in 2007. A charitable foundation she started in 1965 in honor of her relative Rivka Laufer. She called me to review the protocol involving proper dress, speech review and table seating. I must admit that I was totally intimidated by her fierce female force. She was definite, precise, exact and clear with her instructions. I promised that I would behave accordingly and not disappoint her. After all, it was a great honor to be chosen by her. I scoured the stores to come up with just the right suit that sent the message she wanted for her event. Thank G-d, my orange and white brocade Carolina Herrera ensemble met with her approval as was my dvar Torah and guest list selection. When she approached me afterwards with a great and generous hug, I knew that this woman was as genuine as she was fabulous.

Throughout the years, I've had the privilege to hear her speak passionately about her personal journey from the depths of the Holocaust to accomplished businesswoman and extraordinary philanthropist. You can read her book or count the numerous dedication plagues from The Great Synagogue in Jerusalem to institutions and schools throughout New York and beyond.

If she was walking the runway at a fashion event for The Young Israel of Deerfield Beach or giving a lecture for Torah Cafe, she didn't miss a step. Meeting her in the gym at a Passover program involved exchanging weightlifting routines as well as a lecture on calorie intake. She was always perfectly put together in any and every situation well into the years that most would just give up! Which is quite remarkable because sometimes I could barely match my sneakers with my T-shirt. Our last phone conversation, about 5 months before her passing, was mostly about the latest facial cream that her dermatologist gave her. It supposedly makes her look 20 years younger. Believing her was never an issue, as she was more accurate that a beauty magazine.

Yet, the most touching thing she did, I never really shared with anyone. Upon my last divorce, she called me regularly with chizuk (support) and solid advice, always ending the conversation with telling me how beautiful she thought I was.

She was bold, beautiful and empowering, and that's a combination that's quite rare. She wasn't an Instagram influencer with thousands of followers or a social media sensation, she was so much bigger than that.

Although you may believe that the description of her is too gashmiyus, or frivolous, she would think otherwise! In a world of disappearing images of Jewish women from media and shrinking voices in leadership, Fran was a fierce warrior of the complete opposite orientation. She was a magnificent phoenix that rose from the ashes of the WW2 Holocaust Era to soar and blaze a trail for Jewish women everywhere with her brains, beauty and style without any trace of fading into the background of life. I contacted her daughter Gail Laufer Yashar to share my essay for the book. To my delight, here is her reply,

"Thank you for your kind words, warm feelings and personal stories that you shared about our mother, Fran Laufer, A"H

As you said, she was larger than life, and her ebullience, energy and enthusiasm was positively contagious; you felt her when she entered a room, and she captured you with her wise words and counsel. As it takes one to know one, my mother recognized and appreciated strong women who could make a difference, and her friendship with you reflects that you and she were one of a kind.

As you were captivated by her beauty, grace, pragmatism, strength and wisdom, you joined us in regaling the lessons and memories of our precious mom Fran Laufer, a woman committed to remembering her lost childhood while forging ahead purposefully with a lifelong mission-rebuilding and perpetuating the Jewish people!"

We have a lot to learn from little Frimit Of Chrzanow, Poland who grew into Fran Laufer (ZL), the Jewish Icon.

The Exotic Bird

Listening to Iris Apfel describe her high school days in Astoria, Queens, ditching class to go shopping instead, reminded me of my senior year at Bais Yaakov High School of Queens (now Shevach). I was voted "most likely to shop" in my yearbook, because I thought Thursday and Friday afternoons were meant for exploring department stores on 34th street in Manhattan as B. Altman's and Ohrbach's.

I think I found my spirit animal in Iris with every feathered boa, gem studded leather pants, multicolored furs, stacks of dimensional bracelets, cleopatra collars and signature black round eyewear. I am certain that I made the right choice in my selection as I am surely not alone in my sentiments. Ivan Bart, president of IMG Models and IMG Fashion Properties, said, "Iris is an icon with immeasurable talent. She radiates creativity and inspiration, and we are so excited to explore new and unique opportunities with her, where her natural gifts can be shared with the world. At 97 years old, Iris continues to prove that age is just a number and should not be something that defines you."

I cannot tell you how many times matchmakers, good friends and even family would refer to me as "a rare bird" that not many people appreciate and is often misunderstood. Through the years I always wondered if this terminology was a compliment or an act of defiance. Along comes this fashion icon and changes my perception completely.

In 2005, Apfel was the first living person, who was not a designer, to have her clothing and accessories exhibited at the Metropolitan Museum of Art, in an exhibition titled "Rara Avis (Rare Bird): The Irreverent Iris Apfel." The exhibition was so successful it traveled to the Norton Museum of Art in West Palm Beach, FL, the Nassau County Museum of Art in Roslyn Harbor, NY, and later to the Peabody Essex Museum in Salem, MA. The collection will find its permanent home in a dedicated gallery at The Museum of Lifestyle and Fashion in Boynton Beach, FL. The ultimate gesture of appreciation of her eternal style status is her own doll. In 2018,

Mattel created a Barbie doll in Apfel's image, making her the oldest person to ever have a Barbie.

Last year I had the time of my life with her at Bijoux in Palm Beach, FL. The contemporary art jewelry sale at the Armory Art Center featured 36 jewelry artists from around the world, plus Apfel. I could not write up the sales fast enough for the women that flocked to Iris's area. They all wanted a piece of her style. "Did she really wear this?" There were about 300 pieces from her personal collection for sale at the show. A beautiful young woman bought a double peacock enamel neckpiece for $1200 with one condition. She wanted a photo with Iris. They showered her with gifts, paintings, and praise. They told her stories, recommenced doctors, restaurants and manicurists.

She is almost a centenarian woman who started her own textile company, Old World Weavers, in 1950 with her late husband, Carl. Aside from having a hand in nine restoration projects at the White House during her multi-decade career, she has racked up her share of ad campaigns in recent years including Kate Spade, MAC Cosmetics, Alexis Bittar, HSN and more. She has no intention of stopping soon. Listing her accomplishments would take another two pages. There is her book, **Iris Apfel: Accidental Icon** which launched at Bergdorf's last year with her own windows and a pop-up shop. A project with Bernardaud and a collaboration with a glassware company called Nude based in Istanbul. And we cannot forget the award-winning documentary IRIS, and the Apfel Hall at the Costume Institute in the Metropolitan Museum of Art.

I was privileged to have witnessed closeup, the adoration, respect, inspiration, and motivation she provides her fans and audience. She is transcending age to reach generations of people with her extraordinary message of sheer "fabulousness."

I learned a valuable lesson in marketing and branding. Authenticity is the key to success. Iris is what Iris is without filters, fuss, or fakeness. There is a message here that reflects what G-d wants from us daily. Each day is an opportunity to live to the fullest, especially in joy. G-d listens to the prayers of those that live in joy. Iris lives in joy that is channeled through her style, wit, colors, and presence.

At the end of her interview, she said "live everyday like it's your last because one day you will be right."

I flew back home to Kew Garden Hills (Queens) with a renewed sense of self and purpose. I might also be a rare bird but I am going to happily fly every day and appreciate the wisdom of Iris Apfel.

Grande Dame of Rebbetzins

My mobile phone rang at midnight as my daughter invited me to a movie as a distraction from the reality I was facing. It rang again in the theatre, "Hello Tobi, its Rebbitzin Jungreis, how are you feeling?" I ran out of the theatre and continued the conversation in the lobby. I am not going to share the very frank sentiments she expressed as my third marriage and its problems were being played out in the public eye. She insisted that I attend her private classes at her office at Hineni headquarters.

I mustered up the strength to go that week, feeling deeply ashamed of my weak appearance and fear of being recognized as a subject fallen from grace. As I meekly stepped into her office, her face lit up with a big smile. "Sit down momala, everything will be ok." After her wonderful dvar (talk) Torah about the parsha, she mingled lovingly with all the participants as we basked in the warmth of the loving cocoon created by this special Rebbitzen. I walked over to her desk and she put her hands on my head and blessed me with the priestly prayer. I do not remember if I burst out crying or just felt faint, but she summoned two women to take care of me. And they did. Rebbitzen Jungreis recognized that I needed help without me asking. I am so grateful to her for saving my mind and neshama (soul) when I needed it the most.

It is no surprise that she came from a prestigious lineage of rabbis and healers, for she possessed an air of royalty and empathy. Her complete range of spiritual gifts were a rare treasure.

If clothing can describe a person, Rebbetzin Esther Jungreis (ZL) was the Grande Dame of Style. Her look was impeccable and deliberate. Her attention to detail in dress, shoes, hair, and makeup emanated a picture of strength, beauty, self-worth, and purpose. The long white ball gown skirts together, with expertly tailored jackets, balanced by her high heels and delicate jewels, remined me of a Jewish Queen (Malka). She was never had a hair out of place or her face without makeup. She was a constant reminder that Jewish women are graceful beauties without the need for harsh attention. As she approached the podium to speak words of Torah (Bible), I immediately knew exactly what a woman of valor looked like. She was a charismatic speaker and beloved teacher whose enormously popular revival-style assemblies urged secular Jews to study Torah (Bible) and embrace traditional religious values.

She was often called "the Jewish Billy Graham," and her artfully staged rallies, with theatrical lighting and musical accompaniment, were backdrops for her charismatic presence. Her movements and speeches were passionate yet refined. She balanced modesty with excitement in her unique way. She called herself "Rebbetzin," the Yiddish honorific title bestowed on wives of rabbis. Her husband, Rabbi Theodore Jungreis started two congregations.

She founded an outreach organization on the Upper West Side of Manhattan called Hineni. Its name translates from Hebrew to "I am here," referencing Abraham's answer when called upon by G-d in Breishis (Genesis).

This immensely popular organization offers multiple classes in the Torah (Bible) subjects, and social mixers at which Jewish singles can find one another, plus high holiday services. As its leader, Rebbetzin Jungreis addressed large audiences globally with her message of great urgency and hope.

She routinely called the threat of assimilation "a spiritual Holocaust." Living through the concentration camps as a child, she recognized it as a severe threat to present day Judaism. Onstage, she would admonish and warn, then tug at your heart with love and respect which was her masterful plan to engage each mind, soul, and body.

In my humble opinion, her presence in all its components, gave you Emunah (faith). It was her aura of consistent inner and outer beauty that transmitted safety and strength. She conveyed in speech, dress, and manner that you must have faith in G-d. Her commitment to graceful strength impacted the quest for self-growth and empowerment of others. She taught that no matter what happens in life, it is all divinely planned, and it will all work out with adherence to Torah (Bible).

I am curious to know how she would think her legacy has impacted female Jewish leaders. How would she assess the idea that her female image would be eliminated from Jewish advertisements if she were alive today? Or would she instinctively know how to navigate and possibly turn in it another direction? I think she would.

Mothers and Daughters

Upon my daughter's arrival during a very stormy and snowy night on Jan 4, 1994, Dr. Irving Buterman, a 2020 CNN Hero, boldly announced "she's your daughter, Tobi, because she was born with a pearl necklace wrapped around her neck!" Lola Rubinstein was a bit active in the womb and had twisted the umbilical cord around her neck. She recognized my voice immediately because I had been talking to her since discovering she was my baby girl.

Calling her Lola was an absolute decision because we named her after her paternal grandmother who survived the Holocaust. She survived an unimaginably horrific time in The Auschwitz Concentration Camp in Poland. She witnessed her seven-year-old daughter being murdered by the Nazis in the public square of Shainov, Poland. She reinvented her life in the USA with great strength and renewal. It is said that the children of the Holocaust return through reincarnations known as "gilgul or gilgulah" and I have no doubt that my Lola is one of those precious souls. I feel honored and deeply privileged to be a part of the chain of continuation and survival of my people.

A long time ago, I went on the trip of a lifetime. It would be a trip that changed me forever. I was not prepared for the reality that impressed upon me.

In 1993, I escorted Lola's paternal grandfather, Leo Rubinstein (ZL), on a two-week journey to Poland. Growing up in an American Jewish home, I was never affected by the Holocaust directly. This was a sharp contrast to Leo, who survived multiple work camps and the death of his wife and infant daughter. Determined that this would be the adventure of a lifetime, I eagerly awaited seeing Poland through his eyes.

I was not prepared for the shock I felt on the day we went to Auschwitz and Birkenau. My first reaction was to remind myself that I was not on a movie set. The severely harsh reality of these places assaults all your senses. It crushes your sight, smell, sound, touch, and spirit. You are unable to comprehend the cruelty, logistics and order of each block, brick, and door of a death camp. Fighting the urge to scream at every horrific feature, I nearly fainted by the end of the visit. Lola's gracious and heroic grandfather shared endless stories of desperate survival that thankfully led him to his salvation and gave me greater understanding of the people who were prisoners there.

If I could have written a parenting manual called "Do Everything the Opposite of What Your Mother Did," I would have started my first book 27 years ago. However, that is the plan I followed passionately in raising my daughter. Facing all my own trigger points and reversing them to protect my daughter from my past, I finally understood myself as a mother rather than a childhood victim.

Lola, my only child, helped me reverse a pattern that could have been easily passed down from generation to generation. It was a dangerous pattern of mother and daughter relationships that could sometimes be lethal to the soul. Raising Lola, unbeknownst to her, broke the merry go round.

How can I convey her immeasurable influence on me without starting from my very core? My guilt was ever present as I put her through two bad divorces shortly after she turned sixteen. Learning how to forgive myself is among the many items in my shopping cart of emotional issues.

To say that she is the most wonderful thing I have ever created in my life is not true. She is the best thing I have ever been given in my life. G-d created and divinely gifted her to me to nurture throughout her life. I am forever grateful to Him.

I am often in sheer awe of her sensibility and composure, as if I am the child and she is the mother. Her wisdom is far deeper than mine. She is grounded in ways that usually come with years of experience, yet she remains open minded as well. She navigates our ever-changing culture with her with a calmness and grace.

Lola Rubinstein is my daughter, my teacher, my healer, my wonder, my beginning, and my future. Her Hebrew name is Leora, meaning "my light" a name that is perfectly her own.

My Colorful Coat

My colorful coat is sewn together by women (and some men) from the most luxurious and unique fabrics. Each yard is infused with cultural mastery and individual techniques lovingly woven in linens, silks, chiffons, velvets, wools, and cottons from the most exotic resources.

It serves as my shield of protection made of unconditional love. I wear it through the shifting weather conditions as my life changes, passes, and remains in a constant flow of uncertainty.

I could consult with my good friend Donald Levy, whose coat manufacturing companies produce the most popular brands, including Dawn Levy and Moose Knuckles, to teach me a thing or two about the importance of a great coat. However, we must understand that a garment, especially a coat, has its roots in the Torah (Bible).

"And Israel Yaakov (Jacob) loved Yosef (Josef) more than his other sons because he was the child of his old age, and he made for him a "ketonet passim," (a coat of many colors) Bereishit (Genesis 37:3).

Yaakov gave his favorite son a special coat that is described by the Torah (Bible) as a "ketonet passim." The translation of "passim" is shrouded in mystery, and even the word ketonet has various interpretations. It was obviously a very distinctive and special piece of clothing.

Rashi, commentator of Torah (Bible), understands "passim" referring to the fabric from which the coat was made, describing it as "kli milat," based on other statements of Rashi, (Shabbat 54a, s.v. l'milat; Yechezkel 27:18, s.v. v'tzemer tzachar; and Chullin 50b, s.v. makom she'ein), "milat" is understood as clean, white wool (Maharsha, Megillah 16b, s.v. milat; Rashash, Bava Metzia 78b, s.v. batlei). Some others translate passim as a silk garment, (Rav Saadia Gaon; Ibn Ezra to Esther 1:6 in conjunction with Megillah 12a; Rabbi Yosef Chaim miBaghdad [the Ben Ish Chai], Od Yosef Chai, 25a). All suggesting that these materials would be reserved for clothing worn for special occasions.

My colorful and magical coat could have been shredded, rearranged, tattered, or stripped apart, for life can certainly do that to. Yet, mine endured and brightened over the past 62 years, collecting more sparkle and shine on the way. Each of my own cycles welcoming new and unusual designs and replacing the broken threads with new spools of yarn.

More importantly, I need to address the gratitude I have for these skilled makers. Hakarat HaTov (or Hakaras HaTov), is the Hebrew term for gratitude. It means "recognizing the good." Gratitude is the expression of appreciation for what one has been given by family, friends, and G-d. Its value has nothing to do with monetary or a check list of actions. It is measured by the commodity of goodness generated by others through actions of warmth, concern, sympathy, empathy, guidance, help, trust, and love.

Let me introduce you to all the special people that made my coat. They are the most integral part for they are my prayer warriors and G-d's angels on earth. They have collectively and magically given my coat its ability to function, fight, flow, form, and fulfill my mission.

Alvina Alston, CEO of MoreMedia

Astar Nussbaum, Family Member, Special Education Teacher

Betty Makovsky, Family Member

Catherine Underwood, Brand Licensing Executive, Retired VP of Licensing Union Bay, Editor of The House of Faith and Fashion

Ceilee Sitt, Event Planner and Philanthropist

Chanie Einhorn, Real Estate Management

Debra Rabinowitz, Family Member

Donna Schneier, Family Member, Founder of Donna Schneier Fine Arts and Bijoux Contemporary

Dr. Rabbanit Adena Berkowitz, Psychotherapist, Lawyer and Founder of Kol HaNeshmah, Senior Educator at the Manhattan Jewish Experience

Dr. Rachael Shindler, Nutritionist

Elizabeth Sutton, Artist, Entrepreneur and Founder of Elizabeth Sutton Collection

Esther Muller, Senior Global Adviser to Sotheby's International, President of the Academy of Continuing Education, Real Estate

Georgie London, Retired Executive in Communications

Hillary Barr, CEO of R New York Real Estate Brokerage

John Henry Edington III, Makeup Artist and Stylist

Mimixa Patel, Executive Assistant to The House of Fashion and Fashion book projects

Natalie Packer, Owner, Packer Ford and Lincoln Auto

Rebbetzin Leah Rokeach, Therapist

Rebbitzen Miriam Yerushlami, Author, Lecturer and Therapist

Rebbetzin Sara Shulovitz Vorhand, Criminal Attorney, Rebbetzin of the Congregation Heichal Moshe

Rivky Rokeach, Teacher

Shevy Shanik, Founder of Shevy Shanik Events

The House of Faith and Fashion

Abe Roth

Influencers

Chaim Roth

The House of Faith and Fashion

Tobi and Lola Rubinstein by Joan Roth

Photo by Tobi Rubinstein

Fran Laufer

Donna Schneier

THE END IS ONLY THE BEGINNING

"Master of the World, I wanted it to be one way, but I see that Your will is different. I accept your will and thank you for the change in plans," from **The Garden of Gratitude** *by*
Rabbi Shalom Arush.

The End Is Only the Beginning

Tobi Rubinstein

The End Is Only the Beginning

The best way to describe my state of mind right now is through a visual exercise.

Picture yourself standing in a magnificent kitchen. It is filled with finest ingredients on the planet. As you gaze in wonder of this environment, and breathe in the exotic aromas and flavors, you are confounded by what masterpiece to create with them. It represents the amazing cornucopia that G-d has given you.

I have received that gift in fashion, jewelry, art, beauty, style, and now in sickness. I hope to continue this journey with another book through my process of finding G-d in all these magical spaces.

Thank you for visiting The House of Faith and Fashion where I hope to see you again very soon.

Tobi Rubinstein

ACKNOWLEDGEMENT

"Thankfulness has an inner connection with humility. It recognizes that what we are, and what we have, is due to others and above all, to G-d."

Rabbi Lord Jonathan Sacks (ZL).

- Chief Rabbi Pinchus Goldshmidt, Chief Rabbi of Moscow and the President of the Conference of European Rabbis

- Rabbi Shalom Arush, Author, Founder of Chut Shel Chesed Institutions

- Eli Goldsmith, CEO of Unity Inspires Projects

- Rebbetzin Rochie Pinson, Author

- Regina Rubinov and Dimensions Therapy by Yuval Levi

- Yitzy Weinberg

- Rabbi Leibel and Shaina Stolik, Chabad of South Palm Beach

- Uriel Setareh

- The Mauthner Girls, Susan Toline, Debbie Klein, Linda Weiler

- Joan Roth, Photographer

- Amy Martin Friedman, Photographer

- Gedale Fenster, Motivational speaker, Founder and CEO of the People's Insurance Claim Center and Evolutions Treatment Center

- Jean Alerte, Publisher, Citadelle Publishing, Founder of ACA Branding Agency

- Vinnie Posativo, Founder VPE Talent

- Dr Samantha Choen, Alexis Ohara and Mt. Sinai Hospital Staff

- Orner Families, Eli Orner and family, Shimmy, Debra Orner and family, Dr. Gabi and Mindy Orner and family, Dr. Hersh and Dr. Shahnaz Orner, David Orner, Irving Orner and family

- Aryeh Rabinowitz and Family

- Queens Jewish Link

- Rabbi Joseph Issac Korf, Hollywood Community Synagogue, Chabad

- Jody Bauraskas, Diana Myers, Regina Frykman

- RCCS Rofeh Cholem: Yidas Weiss, Pessie Feinstein

- Shainy Batshevah

- Ari Zoldan, CEO of Quantum Media

- Bruce Teitelbaum

- Sharona Abraham, Owner of Sharona's Dough to Go

- Marcos Benzaquen

- Derrick Hammond, CEO of 2020 Vizion Entertainment

Made in the USA
Middletown, DE
28 April 2021